So You Want To Be a Cop...

So You Want To Be A Cop...

A Family and Police memoir

Robert Rattenbury

So You Want To Be a Cop published by Rangitawa Publishing, Feilding, New Zealand 2018.

©Robert Rattenbury

ISBN 978-0-9951046-9-3

www.rangitawapublishing.com

rangitawa@xtra.co.nz

Rangitawa
PUBLISHING

"Defend the weak, protect both young and old, never desert your friends. Give justice to all, be fearless in battle and always ready to defend the right."

The law of Badger Lords" – Brian Jacques

For Jenny, Jodie and Luke – You are my world

Acknowledgements

Sergeant Bill Nicholson of Palmerston North, Police Photographer and fellow AOS member, for providing details and advice on the Tigertooth and Bell Block incidents and the passing of Detective Tony Harrod

Murray Crawford, Whanganui author, for providing me with mentoring as a novice author and for having the patience and kindness to proof read this work prior to publishing.

Caroline Barron of Lovewordsmusic for providing me with much needed advice and support about formatting, them and context.

Russell Colquhoun, Sergeant of Police (Retired), for continually encouraging and supporting me to make a book out of my wee stories.

Kevin McAvoy, Senior Constable (Retired), for offering advice and memories about "Bill".

Harry Quinn, Detective Inspector (Retired) for advice and comment about the Harkin Homicide.

David Whitford, Detective Senior Sergeant (Retired) for advice and comment about the Harkin Homicide.

Rowan Carroll, Director of the New Zealand Police Museum, for providing material for the Morgan shooting and for her kind words of support and encouragement.

My publisher Jill Darragh of Rangitawa Publishing for her support and guidance.

References

- *"Wellington – the Dark Side" pp 17 and 18 – William Minchin (Undated) – Morgan Shooting 1982*

- *The New Zealand Police Association Newsletter 1st December 2012 – Genesis of the Armed Offenders Squad*

- *The NZ Listener – "Spurred to action" - David Lomas 15 January 2011 – Harkin Murder 1983*

Foreward

The Law is a difficult taskmaster. Its principles and their rigid application may lead to injustice.

The concentration, analysis and identification of the facts or factors involved in any incident or the consideration of the elements of any alleged offence require experience and the understanding of fellow citizens. Officers like Rob Rattenbury with coal face experience are best fitted for such decisions.

The essential qualities (to me) of humility, honesty and integrity contribute to the way in which competent Police Constables, Court staff and Judges carry out their obligations and the work assigned to them in the interests of our community.

I have acted for Rob Rattenbury as he mentions. Also I can recall speaking to him after the Wanganui incident with Huey, Dewey and Luey and congratulating him on his ability to fall into a ditch and thus being unable to observe that incident. From memory "you have learned a lot since our last hearing".

It was impossible for me to read this account without tears welling in my eyes from time to time. The many names in this book are real people to me and they sprang to life as I recalled them and my shared experiences with them in Court or otherwise. It would be wrong to mention names in case unintentionally I offend someone by omission.

I must however mention Daphne Pomare. A person of warmth and good humour who made an excellent contribution to Lower

Hutt. Daphne was a strong mentor to young Constables. Of the others without exception I found to be men and women who kept their word and discharged their obligations to a high standard.

Rob's humility, competence and integrity shines through these pages as does his loyalty and devotion to his wife and family and those disadvantaged members of our community who require and deserve our support.

This book is useful on a number of counts. It carries us through his personal development, home life, schooling and in addition it is a more than useful record in historic terms of the places and times that he mentions.

There are a number of points in common between Rob and myself. My hometown is Wanganui . I practised Law in Lower Hutt from 1961 to the late 1970's and I also lived and practised Law in Masterton from 1971 until appointed to the Bench in 1990 at Otahuhu and then Manukau. Also spending some years in Wanganui. I also met the leaders of the dog school when it was in its infancy.

These few words would be incomplete if I did not emphasise that Police personnel accept risk as part of their everyday duties. As those who have been present or heard of various confrontations it is important to remember there is only a fraction of a second with a stab of a knife or the pulling of a trigger to take a life or cause serious injury. Branded on my brain and no doubt on all in the law in Lower Hutt, when in 1963 two constables were shot and killed attending a domestic. The risk of which I speak may be reduced by planning and preparation but risk remains.

There is as great a risk with personal issues. Two such incidents occurred while I was sitting in South Auckland. A very competent male prosecutor and a policewoman (a more than competent witness) took their own lives. These incidents leave us questioning, helpless and sorrowing.

In my view our society is quite violent. I recall a grandson causing major injuries to his grandfather who was going fishing very early in the morning in the far north and had the temerity to enquire where he had been. An innocent member of the public going about his business being knocked to the ground and his head stomped into the asphalt footpath. A solicitor defending a person (a sentenced prisoner) charged with unlawful possession of a firearm calling the partner to give evidence that it was her rifle.

The partner had been assaulted by the defendant. A possible defence certainly. I asked for the rifle to be handed to me thinking I would get the witness to show me how she would remove the bolt. From an abundance of caution (I have a pistol and firearms licence) and no wish to be shot in my own court, I pulled back the bolt to check it was unloaded. To my horror there was a round in the rifle with an indentation from the firing pin on the primer. A reasonable inference being that the witness was lucky she had not been shot by the person she was supporting.

Discussing the potential and actual loss of life brings to mind the current issue of police chases. Somewhere in the equation must be the certainty of detection. This coupled with a balancing of actual and perceived risk.

Finally reading and experiencing the emotions arising from Robs book, it would be wrong of me not to emphasise the shared experiences that he details, the implicit risks, the expression of an independent point of view to a superior, and the development of life-long friendships from these very experiences.. My personal recollection is of his great smile which extended to his eyes. Accordingly I have no hesitation in recommending his book.

We will all be better for this reminder of good values and the life- long experiences he, without reservation, shares with us.

John Clapham

District Court Judge (Retired)

Contents

Foreword

Introduction

1	Some Sad Stories	21
2	Murder Without Remorse	34
3	Family History	38
4	Dad	46
5	Mum	54
6	Growing Up In Naenae	60
7	Primary School and Church Life	65
8	Secondary School	74
9	A New Life – Why the Police	81
10	My First Posting	93
11	Jenny, Her Family and a Wedding	105
12	A Country Life For Me	115
13	How NOT to Plan a Successful Career In The Police	121
14	A Life With Dogs	125
15	Then Life Stands Up And Smacks You Right Between The Eyes	135
16	Sergeant – Bit Of A Change	139
17	There Is Nothing Funny About This Story	143
18	Operation Rugby	149
19	Before The Bench	162
20	Whakapohane	166
21	Pegleg – A Tragedy	170
22	A New Start For Us All	177
23	Bill And Ben The Flower Pot Men	187
24	Some Armed Offender Squad Memories	190
25	Some Interesting AOS Operations	195
26	More War Stories	208

27	Something A Bit Lighter	215
28	Senior Sergeant, Getting A Bit Serious Now	221
29	Another Death Of A Comrade	233
30	Sex Crimes – The Sad, The Mad And The Plain Just Bad	239
31	Police Bars	246
32	Police Partners	250
33	Time To Go	252
34	The Last Instalment Of "My Brilliant Career" Yeh Right.	256

Introduction

For the past ten or so years I have been writing my family history and also decided to add some stories from my time in the New Zealand Police. These scribblings were originally only intended for my children Jodie and Luke so that they have some sense of place in the scheme of things as descendants of 19th century Irish and English settlers in New Zealand but with a connection to Iwi as well.

However I found that as time went on the stories kept flowing in terms of both family and Police tales. I also, either foolishly or otherwise, decided to share some of the stories with extended family, friends and Police, both serving and retired, via Facebook until I had the beginnings of a book.

The feedback from family and friends has been so positive that I have decided to publish the stories in book form. Some of what you read will be shocking, some will be very sad. Most will, I hope, be at least interesting and maybe entertaining. I have spoken a lot about my family and growing up in Naenae in the 1950's and 1960's. This provides a background to what sort of adult I became but also a bit of a social history of the times. You will see that growing up for me had its challenges but I am sure I am no different from thousands of other children of my generation whose parents had grown upin the Great Depression of the early 1930's, in the aftermath of World War 1 when so many of their uncles, older brothers and cousins had died, and then lived or fought in World War 2.

Our parents' generation is nowadays referred to as the Great Generation. This is meant as a compliment to people who had more than their share of woe and sadness to contend with. I believe that this was reflected in the behaviour of a lot of adults I knew as a child and teenager. Many of them were scarred by deprivation and hopelessness during the depression and then the loss of loved ones during the Second World War. I make no excuses for some of the things that happened in my home as a child but do ask that there be an understanding of the background of my parents and their generation. Despite all I loved my parents dearly and unreservedly and I know that they loved me and my siblings.

My policing career was, in most respects, ordinary and without fanfare. I never attained high rank, nor did I seek this. I never had a high profile in the media other than as a Prosecutor, but who reads the Court news. However I was very privileged to be able to work with some of the best people that this country has produced. You will see that I do not suffer fools well and that I am not slow in showing this, mostly, in my younger days, to my own detriment. I made a few enemies in the Police in terms of people who I felt did not measure up to my idea of policing a community of decent law- abiding people. I had no time for people in the Police who sought sinecure positions away from actually dealing with people and crime. That is fine as I knew I was right. I could be abrasive and confrontational as a cop, especially with gangs and certain criminals. In my day a cop could get away with this but frankly guys and girls like me would not last five minutes nowadays.

The New Zealand Police was and is almost a unique Police service in the Western world. It is still, by and large, an unarmed service although access to weaponry is now easier than ever before, for very good reasons. It has been and still is one of the most corruption free Police services in the world. I rate it as the best Police service in the world, mainly due to the quality of people drawn to its ranks and the stringent entry requirements imposed.

You will see the humour, camaraderie and fun of being a cop in the following stories. You will also see the tragedy, sadness and sometimes the hopelessness and the fear involved in policing in New Zealand.

Cops in New Zealand tend to be in my time a hardy lot, fit and healthy, tough as nuts but with a wicked sense of humour, sometimes a bit dark, but very outgoing and not cut off from their communities like some Police services. I am sure the same applies nowadays. They all come from the communities they serve. They are your peers, ex-school mates, ex-work mates, the sons and daughters of people you grew up with, went to school with, work with and played sport with. They may be your own son or daughter.

I was and still am very proud to have been a cop in New Zealand and I would recommend the role to any young person who wants to give back to their community and to make a difference to people in the community who, for whatever reason, cannot look after themselves.

In this book I have changed some names and places to protect the identity of members of the public and Police where I have felt that they do not deserve to be publicly known and possibly slated for past misdeeds or lack of judgement. These people have all, if still alive, got on with their lives, some after paying for past mistakes.

I have also changed some names to protect the reputation and memory of individuals involved who have since passed.

Have a read and enjoy. If you do not generally like cops this probably will not change your mind but it may explain some stuff. Otherwise I hope there is a laugh somewhere in this tome for you.

Robert Rattenbury 2018

Chapter 1

Some sad stories

Police, like all emergency workers and medical staff, deal with death on a daily basis. The Police act as the Coroner's agents in dealing with sudden deaths arising from accidents or criminal acts. They are responsible for reporting to the Coroner all such deaths and holding enquiry into the circumstances. It is one of the least pleasant parts of being a cop.

It is not unusual for young people to join the Police without ever having seen a dead body. Before I joined I had only seen one person who had died, my dear grandmother. Upon being stationed at Lower Hutt in 1971, I would have attended "sudden deaths" at least once weekly as a section cop working around the clock on shifts. Many elderly people tend to pass at night for some reason in my experience so night shifts and early shifts, especially in cold weather, could be very busy.

When someone dies there is a tendency for family and ambulance staff to ring the Police for some reason. Police will always attend and deal with the tragic loss as appropriately as can be. Not all these deaths are reported to the Coroner as many will be certified by the family GP as death due to a known illness or disease. It is important the Police support the family any way that they can, either by something simple as making a cup of tea for them or as complex as tracking down and informing a family member who is overseas of the death of their loved one and providing advice on how they can come home, if needed.

The following sad stories are about some of the scores of deaths I have attended over the years. Names have been changed.

Frank

In the early seventies I served for a while in Masterton. Frank was an elderly gentleman who lived in Masterton and worked at the local picture theatre as an usher. He was very friendly and popular with patrons. He was single but was in a friendship with a woman. The relationship foundered for some reason and Frank found himself living in a bach at the back of a property in Colombo Road, Masterton. One night he decided to take his own life.

He prepared letters to the Police, his lawyer and his lady friend. He then prepared to take his own life by swallowing a mouthful of cyanide paste and shooting himself with a .22 rifle.

The following morning I was called to the address by the occupants of the house in front of the bach. Frank had been found dead on his bed. When I arrived I arranged for a GP to certify life extinct and then completed a scene examination. Frank looked very peaceful but had the cyanide paste in his left hand and the rifle leaning against his right arm. The rifle was cocked with a round in the chamber. He had no visible injuries.

The letters and the paste and rifle suggested that Frank was intending to take his own life. The eventual post mortem examination showed that Frank had simply expired of natural causes. Everyone at the time believed that he died of a broken heart.

Life is not very fair. - Fred –

Fred served in Vietnam as a professional infantry soldier, surviving that waste of a war intact and returned to New Zealand to his family and discharge from the Army.

Fred loved to hunt and one weekend in 1973 he and a mate decided to go deer hunting in the Orongorongo ranges behind Wainuiomata

Late on the Saturday afternoon myself and another Constable, Ian Weston, were called to the Orongorongo Park as a hunter had been reported shot and assistance was needed to carry him out of the bush. By the time we got to Fred he had died. He had survived war to come home to be shot in his own country by another hunter mistaking him for a deer. This was very tragic for all involved. The shooter was subsequently charged in Court with the relevant offences.

Coincidentally Fred's family lived over the road from Jenny's parents in Masterton and the offender lived not a 100 yards from my parents' place in Naenae.

Dealing with the passing of children is heart-wrenching and gutting every time.

Angel

In 1980 I was on patrol in Stokes Valley early one Saturday evening when I was called to a flat near George Street to a sudden death. Upon arrival I found two young parents terribly upset, being comforted by friends and neighbours.

Their five year old daughter Angel had gone to the toilet and just passed away. She was otherwise a very healthy and bubbly little girl so her death was totally unexpected.

I spent a lot of time with the parents and then took Angel from the home, undertaking the mortuary procedure that had to be done.

When completing my report I realised that Angel was born the same day as my daughter Jodie, exactly the same age. It made me cry.

As a young section cop and again as a Sergeant in charge of young cops I often had to attend the "cot death" of babies, known today as Sudden Infant Death Syndrome. It is hard to describe in words the total devastation and misery felt by young parents when a normally healthy baby passes away suddenly while in his or her crib or cot. As a young father I found this particularly difficult to deal with. I would spend as long as possible with the parents and make sure that older family members were called and were present before the Police departed. I never left parents on their own, after removing the wee one on behalf of the Coroner.

I would also arrange for their priest or minister or holy man to arrive as well in order to help provide some solace for the parents if they were religiously inclined. There is no easy normal way of dealing with such tragedy and I tended to go with what felt right at the time.

One of the most tragic deaths I attended, if there is such a scale for children dying, was the death of a small baby who had been lying on the parents' double bed with his Dad for an afternoon sleep. The father, a big man, rolled over onto the baby while asleep and smothered the child. The father was Pakeha and the mother Maori. They would not let us take baby away from the house for some hours. I managed to convince them that we had to do this but that I would only be taking baby to the mortuary which was over the back fence in the Hutt Hospital grounds. I also had to be aware of the cultural feelings involved. The father was utterly despondent and simply did not know what to do with himself. He felt very guilty of course. They had no other children, having just recently started their family. I do not know how I would have coped if I had been him.

I learned that it was ok and appropriate to cry with the parents in these circumstances. It was not hard to do believe me. At the same time taking charge is also required in a very sensitive way.

When love goes wrong

Through my Police service I was involved in quite a few homicide enquiries, some of which made the national news and others not so much. The following three stories are tragic to say the least. They are about people killing the one person in their lives they, perhaps, loved the most. Again I have not used real names as the people charged may still be alive. I am still friends with one of the persons. She has since led a very quiet and respectable life as a mother raising and providing for a great family.

Jim

Jim was a carpenter who lived in Masterton while I was stationed there in the early 1970's. He was a quiet, thoughtful and thoroughly decent man. He was also a very proud Maori. Jim was estranged from his first wife and had formed a relationship with a Pakeha woman. She lived in a unit in Cameron Block, a rough state housing area in Masterton and had a reputation. However Jim saw past this and loved the woman. Over time he found out that she was being unfaithful to him.

When Jim was next in Wellington he called into an Army Surplus store and purchased a Lee Enfield bayonet. One evening, Christmas Eve if I recall right, upon his return to Masterton by railcar, he broke into the woman's home while she was out and awaited her return. Upon her return he stabbed her to death and then tried to take his own life with the bayonet, as well. I was working at the time with another junior Constable, Kevin McAvoy. Mac and I had gone through training together. We only had two man shifts those days and for some reason we had no Sergeant working. I was watch house keeper so could not leave the station as we had a 111 line and some prisoners in the cells. Mac and I called out staff, including the CIB, and set up an operations base, sending the only other cop available at short notice, Kevin Whiteman to the scene with Civil Defence Policeman, Sonny Lusty, to attend. Kevin did a very good job holding the scene while we organised matters.

Jim survived but, following surgery, I sat with him for several shifts in case he wanted to make a dying declaration as he was not that well and may not have pulled through. I got to know Jim quite well. After a few days it was clear that Jim would survive his self-inflicted injuries and he was subsequently charged with murder. I still carried on guarding him now as he was a prisoner. We got to know each other quite well and I was impressed by the basic goodness of the guy. He was just an ordinary bloke who did not know what to do in very trying circumstances. I do not for one second condone what he did but it showed me the strength of human passion and the ease with which we, as humans, can kill if provoked beyond what is personally bearable. Jim was very remorseful for causing the death of his lover, spending a lot of time in tears for her. He loved her but she did not seem to understand the depth of his love.

When he was discharged from hospital I escorted him to Mt Crawford prison in Wellington where he was placed on remand awaiting his Court hearings and trial. In those days escorts were normally done by rail. Jim and I sat in the guard's cabin on the railcar to Wellington for several trips back and forward over subsequent months and Court hearings in Masterton. Because he was handcuffed to me the NZR did not want him sitting in the general seating area for some reason. Those old Fiat railcars were not the most comfortable trains to ride in in the baggage area of the Guards cabin, we had to take turns sitting and, being summer in the Wairarapa, it was as hot as Hades in the cabin.

As I said Jim was depressed and despondent about what he had done. He subsequently appeared in the Wellington High Court and was, following trial, discharged on the
murder charge but convicted of manslaughter. He was sentenced to three years in prison. Upon his release he carried on living a quiet life.

Kay

Kay lived with her husband and children on the Western Hills in Lower Hutt. She ran her own business and her husband owned a very well-known and successful family business in Lower Hutt. They were a wealthy and very social couple and very well-known in the Lower Hutt business community. Outwardly the family was great but what transpired showed that Kay lived in constant fear of her husband.

One cold winter Saturday night in 1980 the couple attended a social function at a local golf club. They travelled in the husband's utility vehicle. During the evening, following a decent ingestion of alcohol Kay's husband became upset with her for some reason. He was seen by others to lose his temper with her, carry her to his utility and throw her in the tray of the vehicle, driving off with her hanging on. Kay was only wearing a formal evening dress. A short time later I was sent to their home by our Control staff following Kay's mother ringing 111 to say that there had been a stabbing. Kay had rung her. Upon arrival at the home I saw Kay through the kitchen window standing at the sink. She appeared stunned and confused. Upon entering the house I saw a bloodied Wiltshire Stay Sharp knife in the sink. I took Kay away from the sink and the knife, sat her down in the dining room and I had a Constable sit with Kay, able to take notes of anything Kay said. I then searched the house as no one else appeared to be home. In the main bedroom I found the naked body of a male on the floor by the bed with one stab wound in the chest. Life was extinct. The smell of fresh blood and death was noticeable and unpleasant.

I called the ambulance and a doctor and arranged for the scene to be guarded pending CIB arrival, sitting with Kay. Not a lot was said at the time but she appeared dishevelled and bruised and did not seem to be in touch with what was going on around her, a matter I later testified to in court.

Kay was subsequently charged with murder and acquitted. From memory her lawyers used the legal defence of automatism and also self-defence. Kay's husband had been beating her and she just used the knife to make him stop. Kay was rational enough to call her mother after the event but was in a very detached state when we arrived, staying that way for quite a while, not really sure about where she was or what she had done. There was evidence given about his violence towards her earlier in the evening at the golf club.

The family was very well-to-do and outwardly quite normal in every way except Kay was a beaten and abused wife.
The deceased's family took the result very badly as would be expected.

Kay carried on living and working in the Hutt after the trial, slowly putting her life back together.

Aroha

Aroha was an eighteen year old girl from a very respectable Maori family in a small country town. She was living with her boyfriend Bernard, a Pakeha also from a very respectable home. Bernard was in his mid-twenties and had a very secure career. They had just had a baby girl. Bernard was very keen on his hunting and fishing, activities he undertook with male friends. Aroha was not involved in these activities although Bernard did show her how to load and use a shotgun.

They were in every way a decent hardworking couple. However, Bernard had decided that he did not want to remain in the relationship but that he wanted to travel to the USA on a hunting and fishing trip, leaving Aroha and the baby in New Zealand. On Xmas Eve 1987 Bernard visited his family for a get together, bringing some Xmas cake home for Aroha. Upon his return to their rented home Aroha shot him with his shotgun once in the chest, killing him instantly.

At the time I was attached to the CIB and became involved in the subsequent homicide enquiry. Upon arrival at the home we found Bernard lying on the lounge floor dead and a shot gun and ammunition bandolier on the settee. Aroha was present and, obviously, very upset. Again the unmistakeable smell of death and blood permeated the room tainted with the smell of gunpowder.

Aroha appeared in shock and did not really know what had happened.

Aroha was subsequently charged with murder and, following trial, was acquitted. A lot was made of her youth and the sense of abandonment she faced with the subsequent shame brought on her family. Aroha clearly loved Bernard a lot and did not have the life experience to handle the upcoming desertion. Aroha has gone on to have a family with the wider support of her whanau and is a delightful and hard case woman nowadays.

Bernard's family was disgusted with the verdict which, again, is understandable. I really feel for them. They still live in the small town and I am sure it galls them to see Aroha or her family around and about.

These cases can only be regarded as tragedies. None of the perpetrators were or are criminals. The victims were their lovers, for good or bad. It shows how love can turn bad very quickly.

Death of a comrade

One Saturday evening in late September 1976 I was at home in Wainuiomata looking after our baby daughter Jodie while Jenny was working a half shift at Hutt Hospital. The Evening Post newspaper arrived at about 5.45 p.m. I was deeply shocked to read the headlines about Constable Peter Murphy being shot dead on duty in Invercargill while he was attending a burglary at a local sports shop. It was a fluke shot fired by the burglar who had stolen a rifle and ammunition from the shop and Peter was simply in the wrong place at the wrong time. Of all the mates I have lost over the years this was the unfairest, if that is possible. The person who did it is now walking the streets a free man after serving a "life" term for murder but Peter's family still remember him and mourn him every day.

Peter Murphy was a neat guy. He had joined the Police and was doing his recruit training when he turned up one day for station duty when I was stationed in Masterton about 1974-75.

His brother Mike was a Constable in Masterton. I had gone right through school with Mike, whose family also comes from Naenae. Peter was a few years younger than us and it was a real pleasure to see him in the Police.

Upon graduating from the Royal New Zealand Police College Peter was posted to Invercargill. I remember Peter the day he started school at St Bernadette's convent school as a five year old in my sister's class.

Attending the funeral of a fallen colleague, killed in the line of duty is mind-numbing. The grief shared with, sometimes, hundreds of other Police affects one deeply. This is when you see the worst and best of the Police culture. You do not want to do it too often.

Peter was brought home and buried in Taita Cemetery in Naenae after a Requiem Mass at St Bernadettes. Hundreds of Police attended the funeral.

Peter's family was well-known and highly respected in Naenae so there were also many locals who paid their respects as well, including many of my old school mates from St Bernards College, Peter's old school.

Informing:

One duty I dreaded but steeled myself to do throughout my service was the duty of personally telling someone that their loved one has died and will not be coming home. I did this too many times to count. I have had to tell parents on several occasions that their dear child has been killed in a motor accident after I had spent the previous hour or so extricating the body from the wreck with the help of the Fire Brigade.

I had to tell a woman that her husband was not coming home as he had died of a heart attack on a business trip to Taupo. I did not tell her that he died during sexual intercourse with his secretary. Some things are best left unsaid. The woman was totally devastated by the news obviously. It was not my role to complicate matters for her.

I have told fellow Police friends that a loved one has died, watching the sadness flood their eyes after initially welcoming me into their home for what they thought was a social visit then putting in place help for the cop and his or her family to get home or contact other relatives.

I have sat with families for hours after such jobs, making tea and contacting relations for them if they wanted me to. I also arranged for relations living overseas to be notified using Interpol. Somewhere in the world a cop, just like me, was going to have to go to the home of a child or sibling of someone who had died in New Zealand to tell them the news no one ever wants to hear. That cop would be having the same hole in the pit of his or her stomach as they did this, wishing that they were anywhere else but there in that moment of time.

Many parts of the art of policing are universal and this is one of them unfortunately.

Chapter 2

Murder without Remorse

During my time in the Police I attended or worked on several homicide enquiries. A factor that seemed to come through with most of these crimes when the offender is spoken to is the expression of remorse for either the deceased or at least for the offender's actions and the likely term of imprisonment facing them.

However many kill without any remorse whatsoever. One Sunday afternoon in March 1983 I was at home off duty gardening when I was called out to a homicide enquiry after a male body was found on the shoreline of the Hutt River in Moera, near the pipe bridge crossing the Hutt River.

Upon arrival at the Hutt station I was put in charge of a group of Uniform Branch Constables and tasked by Detective Inspector Colin Lines with doing area enquiries in the Moera suburb. In any serious crime, especially a "whodunit" type crime the Police will always canvass the neighbourhood around the crime scene to obtain any information from members of the public that could lead to the identity and location of the person responsible.

The Homicide Team already had a name and a "mug shot" photo of a suspect. This was a great help for our Area Enquiry Team.

The circumstances of the crime are appalling.

The victim was a young storeman Mark Harkin. He had met his three killers in the public bar of the Hutt Park Hotel in Moera on Saturday evening and began drinking with them. They were unemployed youths, Hemi Reha, Paul Manihera and a sometime ship-girl Esther Solvoll.

Reha had been in the Hutt Valley for a few months, from Hawkes Bay, looking for work. At that time work was difficult to get in the area with many of the large factories in the area closing, especially the car factories.

Manihera was a country boy from Ruatahuna where horses were the preferred method of conveyance. He still had his spurs with him on the evening. He was also unemployed.

Solvoll was Manihera's girlfriend and had been working the boats as a ship girl out of Wellington.

All were short of money and welcomed Harkin to their table in the pub. They did not know him at all. During the evening Reha decided to rob Harkin and kill him, pushing his body into the Hutt River, hoping it would drift out to sea. He shared his plan with the other two when Harkin was in the toilet. They agreed that Solvoll would ask Harkin to take her down to the nearby riverbank for sex, on the way, stopping at the I Fry takeaway bar for some food. Manihera and Hera would follow them at a distance. Solvoll and Harkin duly left the hotel, went to the takeaway bar in a nearby cul-de-sac, Croft Grove, and purchased an eggburger and chips for $1.85, paying for it with a $20 cheque Harkin cashed.

They then walked to the end of the cul-de-sac and up onto the stop bank bordering the Hutt River. Once they were away from the light of the street Reha and Manihera caught up with them and attacked Harkin – the following is an excerpt from Reha's statement admitting the murder.

"Paul grabbed him from behind ... I punched him quite a few times in the face and the stomach ... I started kicking him in the head ... I had the spurs in my pants pocket ... I tried to cut his throat ... I tried using both of my hands and digging it down into his throat ... it didn't work so I kept on kicking ... I took off his belt. I whacked the belt across him but that didn't work ... I wrapped the belt around his head and started pulling ... I was standing on his head pulling the belt tight ... I got Paul to go over and pull the other side ... his head was in the water so I stuck my foot on top of his head ... I took my foot off and pulled up his head with my hand ... I did this just to have a look at him ... I put my foot back on his head."

After killing and robbing Harkin and leaving his body in the water on the edge of the river the three left the scene, Solvoll and Manihera went home and had sex. Reha went to a party where he met a woman and he, too, had sex. A fun night was had by all.

The tide did not take Harkin's body out to sea. It was found the next morning by a fisherman and the Police were called.

We started our area canvass in the late afternoon. In the early evening Constable Mike Glenday interviewed a woman in the flats opposite the takeaway bar. She was the owner of the takeaway. The woman recognized Harkin from previous dealings she had had with him at the burger bar and found his cheque in her takings from the previous night.

This information enabled the Suspect Team under Detective Sergeant Kevin Kalff to narrow down the identity of all three offenders, particularly Solvoll, from talking to patrons in the bar. At 8.00 a.m. the following morning my team went with the Suspect Team to an address in the nearby Moera flats, a large multi-storeyed tower block a short distance from the pub, and executed a search warrant. We found Harkin's cheque book in a drawer in Solvoll's flat.

The three were then taken into custody and subsequently charged with Harkin's murder. At the time I was a prosecutor and I had to race back to the station as I was due to take Court at 10.00 a.m. that morning. I had the pleasure the next day of requesting that the Court keep all three offenders in custody pending trial when they appeared following their interviews.

They all admitted their parts in the killing and did not seem to have any remorse whatsoever. Nor did they express any concerns about their own future, they just seemed numb people. The two men pleaded guilty to murder and Solvoll pleaded not guilty but was found guilty at trial.

I often wonder how Harkin's family coped with his death and what became of the three young offenders. They would all have served their "life" sentences by now and be back in their communities.

Reference: the NZ Listener - Spurred to action, David Lomas 15 January 2011

Chapter 3

Family History

I was born the eldest child of Mary Kathleen Knox and Ronald William Rattenbury in Lower Hutt Hospital on 22 May 1952. My parents were not married at the time, a fact I discovered when assigned to bigamy inquiries in the mid-1970s whilst working as a trainee detective in the Wellington Police Criminal Investigation Branch. Being naturally nosy I looked my own birth certificate up and found it was endorsed with the word "illegitimate" in brackets after my name. Mum and Dad did not bother me with this trifle as a child and it had no impact on my upbringing at all, apart from a little distance displayed by certain relations and family friends. I put this down to the fact that I was regarded as "spoiled" by some adults and generally annoying and noisy by others.

My parents eventually married in February 1954 just before my sister Gail was born and went on to have four more children—Lynne, Sarahlee, Mark and Stephen. As Mum, a Catholic, had married a non-catholic divorcee the Catholic Church decided to excommunicate her from receiving the sacraments. This did not stop Mum from having us all baptised as Catholic and attending Mass as kids. In later life, after Dad divorced Mum, the church dropped the excommunication order and Mum resumed attending Mass and receiving communion. Her love for her church was greater than the Church's love for her.

My poor sister Gail suffered a terrible head injury at birth which resulted in her being very severely brain damaged. She could not walk properly until about the age of seven, could not talk properly and never grew to her milestones. Gail spent from the age of seven years in care, first at Templeton in Christchurch and then the Kimberley Centre near Levin. When Kimberly closed Gail went into shared community housing in the Hutt Valley where she still resides.

The effect of Gail's injury on our family life was devastating to say the least. Mum had a further four children while trying to care for Gail which very nearly put her into care as well.

ACC not exist when Gail was born. Family with children who had suffered traumatic brain injury at birth were left to their own devices. There were facilities and institutions for these children to go to but help in the home was non-existent. Mum had to cope with trying to care for Gail who was very disabled and demanding, as well as care for three other very small children, Lynne, Sarah and Mark. Nowadays my family would have received a daily 24-hour care package for Gail with a support team in situ to help Mum. Assistance would also be given for housing modification, adaptive technology for Gail, speech language therapy, and the purchase of a suitable vehicle to transport Gail around in. There would be respite care for Gail to be looked after while Mum and Dad had a break and Gail would have a lifelong payment of weekly compensation due to loss of potential earnings caused by injury.

After my police life I joined ACC and ended up specialising in the case management of clients with traumatic brain injury, this becoming a bit of a passion. Probably arising from the hurt, stress and neglect my family suffered when Gail was little. This was not the intended plan when I began at ACC but it was identified by my managers that I had the patience and resilience to work with these clients and their families who live with huge stress in their daily lives. I made sure that all my clients and their families were able to access the help that ACC could offer, getting myself offside with ACC management at times for being a bit generous. My reply was simple— how would you cope on a daily basis with a family member who is profoundly affected by brain injury.

No answer— too hard.

I grew up with the Knox family and Mum's cousins the McHughs being the main influence in my life which was, in many parts, wonderful. I remember many happy occasions as a child spending time with my cousin at various places, especially my grandmother's in Waterloo. From the age of ten I attended school with my Knox cousins, Kevin and Chris. I really liked my aunties and uncles on the Knox side but did not really get close to many of my Rattenbury family except for my paternal grandmother Sarah and Dad's brother Uncle Joe and his wife Aunty Barbara in Urenui. Dad was close to Uncle Joe but did not have much to do with his other siblings. I have very distant memories of meeting uncles and aunties on this side but they have never been involved in my life at all.

I have always been very independent and done things my way, a trait that mother instilled in all of us from a young age. I am also blessed with the ability to not need the constant presence of others to make my life interesting and full. In other words I have always been happy in my own company, perhaps the throwback to being virtually an only child some years due to the subsequent gap in ages to my siblings.

My mother used to worry about me being a little lonely as a child and, to help matters I got a dog when I was five. I had always been scared of dogs so this helped overcome that particular phobia. I lost interest in the dog as I grew older and it was given away.

As I said Mum was Roman Catholic of Irish extraction, her grandparents arriving from Ireland and England in the late 19th century. We were all, except Stephen and Gail, educated at primary school level by the Church. Dad was a Christian of indeterminate faith, of Maori and English descent. Although all but Stephen and Gail attended Catholic primary schools I was the only child to attend a Catholic college. More about that later.

My paternal great-grandfather James Rattenbury was born in North Devon at Iddesleigh, in 1840 and came to New Zealand after 1851 but before 1861 as he disappears off the English census then. He farmed as a very young man in and around New Plymouth and found his way into the Militia in the New Zealand land wars. He is reported to have been a bullock driver and for this, received the New Zealand medal late in the 1920s, not long before his death. This means he was at some time or other, under fire during the fighting in the 1860's. There is no record of him receiving the medal but family letters show he did receive it. It had originally been minted for another soldier, a Maori who fought for the Imperial forces but who never uplifted the medal for some reason.

James married Hannah Sampson and his brother Henry married her sister. The Sampson's came from Netherbury in Dorset, near Lyme Regis. James and Hannah had many children of whom my grandfather Louis was one. Louis became a builder and married Sarah Emily Bertrand, a Ngati Mutunga woman from Urenui. They had a long and happy life together raising Dad and his siblings.

The most famous person I recall is an ancestor was Lt. Colonel George Bertrand, my great uncle, who was second in charge of the 28th (Maori) Battalion at the initial formation of the battalion during World War II. He was a territorial soldier and high school teacher who was also in the Pioneer Battalion in World War I. He was my grandmother's older brother.

Sarah Bertrand's parents were Toroa Ika Wairangi and George Bertrand senior. Toroa left George when Sarah was a child and moved to the Chatham Islands where I am told she had another family. Dad recalled meeting her when he is a boy but had little to do with her. She is buried in Karori Cemetery with a descendant.

George Bertrand senior was also in the land wars but may have been in an army regiment rather than the local militia. He is mentioned on occasion as one of the soldiers involved in the famous raid on the Peach Orchard near New Plymouth in about 1860, leading to further fighting between the British Army and local Maori. This may or may not be fact. When checking I could find no record of him receiving the New Zealand medal issued to all Imperial soldiers who came under fire in the Land Wars. He later became involved in local affairs and owned land inland from Waitara. Bertrand Road in Waitara is named after him. It appears that he lived with Sarah and Louis in his home at Urenui in his later years.

James Rattenbury was also involved in local body politics, serving on the Clifton Road's board. James and George would no doubt have known each other well. My paternal grandparents, Lewis Rattenbury and Sarah Bertrand, lived most of their lives in Urenui, North Taranaki. They raised Dad and his five siblings in the house that Sarah's father George Bertrand had built on Schnapper Flat, near the mouth of the Urenui river. Urenui is a beautiful part of the country and is now a very popular holiday and camping site. By the time I was born they had shifted to a small cottage in Takapuna, Auckland, just on the beach front it was a very quiet neighbourhood in the fifties but is now a multi-million-dollar property area.

One of my first memories is travelling on the overnight express with Mum, Dad and Gail to Auckland, crossing the harbour by ferry staying at Grandma and Grandad's home, meeting my Rattenbury cousins who lived nearby. I was about three or four at the time. This was the only time I met my Granddad and I do remember him being the quiet kindly old chap who was building a small (in my young eyes huge) rowing boat in the backyard. Grandma was very affectionate and loving and I felt very much at home with them.

Grandma was thirteen years younger than Grandad and there is a family story that she was supposed to marry an older Maori man for tribal family reasons but she did not like the idea of an arranged marriage and certainly did not like the old bloke she was expected to bed down with so she married Louis, a nice gentle Pakeha bloke who was the village builder and who did not smoke or drink alcohol. The marriage worked, they were devoted to each other and together for over fifty years before Louis died in 1963 at the age of eighty three, raising six children. Grandad worked as a builder until he was seventy five, retiring to carry on building boats in his backyard. After he passed Dad inherited a lot of his carpentry tools, some of which I still have and use. They would be around one hundred and twenty years old by now but still work fine.

Grandma used to travel a bit between her children's homes around the North Island, especially after she was widowed and we did see a bit of her in Naenae. When small I remember her as a very dark women dressed in black. Grandma was Maori but she did not wear black that often and was a very sunny and woman but she could give a good telling off when needed. She had very long black hair until old age but always kept it in a bun. She was staying at our place once when I was small and came out of her bedroom in her dressing gown and with her hair down. It frightened the life out of me. I did not recognise her until she laughed and hugged me.

She always remembered our birthdays and Xmas with a letter arriving with the customary ten shilling note neatly folded inside. After Grandad died a decision was made in the family that Grandma would live in turn with her six children as part of their families. Dad was not keen on this but Mum looked forward to it as she and Grandma got on like a house on fire. When our turn came the old man stacked such an act that Grandma left after a week or so.

We were very upset as we loved her and there was no issue with her living with us apart from her telling Dad to stop drinking so much and to act better as a husband and father. As mother and son they just did not seem to get on. Dad moaned to Mum that Grandma would cost too much to feed. She was a little old lady and Mum was feeding five growing kids at that stage so there was always plenty of food available. Mum gave Dad a speech about Grandma being his mother and to be more understanding. Grandma must have overheard this conversation as the next thing she was walking back from the Rata Street shops with a sack of spuds, vegetables and groceries.

Dad was in the dog-box for quite a while with Mum after this episode. Mum would bring it up every now and again over the years just to let Dad know he was not forgiven for the way he treated his mother.

We continued to see Grandma over the years. She was always interested in what I was up to, generally approving. The last time I saw her was in 1978 when I was a dog handler working on the Royal Tour of the Queen of the Netherlands, Queen Beatrix. I was in Hamilton working when I called in to the rest home Grandma was living in. We spent quite some time together. She would have been eighty five years old then but still in good health, cracking jokes and telling me stories about my Rattenbury cousins, most of whom I did not know or had not seen in many years, but that was alright.

Grandma passed away peacefully in early 1981. My sister Sarah, Grandma's namesake, Jenny and I intended travelling to Hamilton for her funeral but the car broke down at Taihape, blowing a head gasket so we never got to say goodbye to a lovely, noble and caring old woman who we all loved dearly. At the time Dad was newly married to his latest wife and seemed relieved when I rang him to say that we could not make it. He did not really want any of his Lower Hutt family present for some reason.

Chapter 4

Dad

Dad grew up in Urenui, a small village 16 km north of Waitara. His father Louis was the village builder and his mother Sarah spent some time working in the little library but was otherwise a stay at home Mum. Grandad helped build the Waiouru Military Camp at the start of the Second World War. He would have been sixty odd then, born in 1880. Dad and all his siblings went to Urenui School. I do not know much about his upbringing as he never discussed it other than to say his father and mother were teetotal and did not smoke.

Dad left home young and worked on farms until when he was sixteen he joined the Post Office as a cadet. He told me he never attended secondary school. My mother also never had the benefit of a secondary education, leaving school at twelve to help care for her younger siblings while my grandmother Josephine worked. My maternal grandparents separated when my mother was a teenager but they never divorced, likely due to their Catholicism. No benefits in those days so Nana had to work.

Dad served as a soldier overseas in the New Zealand Army and Tongan Defence Force in WW 2 reaching the rank of Sergeant and married a Commissioned Officer, Janet Crompton. After two children, Peter and Rex, this marriage foundered in the late forties. Because of the then divorce laws I arrived well before Dad's four-year separation was up and the divorce was completed. I never met Peter until we were all well into late middle age as Dad severed all contact with his first wife and the boys. I had met Rex in the early 1980s when he and his wife Pat came to a family gathering at my sister Lynne's in Pukerua Bay. Both brothers have lived in Australia for many years and we still have contact, which is great.

Dad served in the Islands from about 1940 to 1943, spending time in Tonga, Fiji and New Caledonia before coming home to New Zealand to retrain prior to going to North Africa and Europe as a member of the reinforcements for the 2nd Division. Dad told me he had suffered injuries either in the islands or during training at Trentham dropping a 44 gallon drum on his feet, crushing them a bit. He recovered and returned to full duties, leading his section of young soldiers as their Sergeant. From all accounts he was a popular and very good NCO and was very close to his guys. He told me that on the day of embarkation from Wellington for Egypt he was stood down from leaving due to his foot injuries. He was retained in New Zealand until the end of the war as an instructor at Trentham Army Camp.

This was, for our sake as children, fortuitous, as Dad explained that in the first action his old section encountered against the Germans they were wiped out to a man. He felt guilty about this for most of his life as he felt that had he been there, they may not have died.

My Dad was a complex man. A part Maori who never really got to grips with his culture although he knew a lot about it. Dad was a man who, I believe, under-achieved all his life. He was incredibly intelligent but never really got the break. Dad had a great future in Government Service. After the war he had to sit three years of exams in one year. He did this, topping New Zealand. He blamed the requirement to do this study to retain his position in the service, to some extent for the failure of his first marriage.

Having found and met my half-brother Peter, who lives near Woollongong, NSW, and discussed this I am not sure. This may have been a factor but it appears that Dad and Janet were doomed from the start due to a difference in class, race, education status and background. Janet came from an affluent upper middle class background with a very sound private education for a woman of her class, whereas Dad never made it to secondary school and grew up in a small Taranaki village as a "half caste". He was very intelligent and a hard worker but I believe he lacked confidence at times.

I used to see this a lot as a child, usually expressed in drunken outbursts at Mum accompanied often with physical violence towards her. – Like it was Mum's fault.

Dad left the Post Office at the time his first marriage ended and spent the rest of his working life in factory jobs or clerical jobs, working long hours to make a living and operating well below his potential which he found quite frustrating.

Mum put up with Dad for about twenty eight years. Dad was a great father to me, especially when I was little, a distant father to his daughters and came to ignore Mark and Steven. He slowly became distant to me over the years as well, especially after I married. I am not sure why. All three of us boys tried to please Dad but this never seemed to work. Mark adored Dad as a young boy but when he became a teenager Dad used to ridicule him and berate him for whatever shortcomings. Mark felt these barbs deeply and came to despise Dad. Despite Dad's coming and goings and the arguments I do remember both Mum and Dad showing a great deal of affection for each other and for us as wee kids. We knew we were all loved.

Whilst we never really went without, we never had holidays as kids apart from the odd weekend trip to Urenui to see Uncle Joe or day trips to Kimberley Hospital near Levin to see my sister Gail who went there when she was about eight and remained a resident until it closed. Dad would be at the RSA every night of the week and on both days of the weekends. Mum did not socialise with his club mates, which was a cause of some disharmony. Mum's dad Alf was apparently an alcoholic and I think she saw this in Dad's friends and came to see it in Dad.

When Mum and Dad separated in about 1980 Mum told me that Dad was "queer", the term then used for homosexual. This surprised me as I had thought, when a teenager and more aware of things, that he played around but not that he was gay. There used to be a lot of nights when Dad simply did not come home from the pub or left after dinner and did not come home until a day or so later. This seemed to be understood by my mother because when we got upset about this as kids she would tell us not to worry, that Dad would be home tomorrow. After having eight children and re-marrying another woman after divorcing Mum I guess Dad may actually have been bisexual. – I am not sure as I am not an expert on homosexuality by any means.

How did I feel about Dad being gay? I was shocked and sad for him really. He was still my father and was basically a very good man and I still loved him as my father. It certainly made no difference to my feelings for the "Old Man". Mum told me the names of his gay friends, most of whom I knew and looked up to as a young man. All these men were married and outwardly "respectable" in the area I grew up in. Some were actually family friends who we saw often growing up. One acted as my referee when I applied to join the Police.

I cannot imagine the hurt and distress that both my parents went through due to this, both having to live a double life. Being gay or bisexual prior to 1986 was a crime in New Zealand. It was also, in many circles, a very shameful thing to be. I know that Dad had a friend Geoffrey that used to visit us when I was small, a very dapper, well-dressed chap who was exceedingly kind to Mum and me. According to my sister Sarah this was the chap Dad was living with when Mum was pregnant with me. Mum told Sarah that when she discovered she was pregnant with me she visited Dad at a flat in Epuni where he was living with Geoffrey, told Dad and asked him to make a choice.

I cannot imagine the life my poor Dad had to endure due to this. No wonder he was unhappy a lot of the time.

I often wonder what would have happened if Dad had not chosen to be with Mum. I assume I would have been bought up by Nana in Waterloo with Mum continuing to work. There was certainly no question of my being adopted out of the family. The Irish Catholic tradition of family is too strong for this to be considered, very similar to the Maori concept of whanau. The downside of this would have been not having my siblings I guess.

With what I have learnt about drinking I am sure Dad was an alcoholic and suffered depression for many years. He could never tell any of us how pleased he was with our efforts at anything. When other kids were going away on holidays with their families we stayed at home as Dad had stuff at the RSA club to do. I had my first family holiday when I was sixteen. We spent a week in a cottage in Raumati.

To be fair to Dad he did try. He would come to watch me play rugby a lot when I was at secondary school and was instrumental in me playing club rugby at fifteen for his old club Hutt Old Boys. I was an average rugby player at best and I think this disappointed him. I was happy. I enjoyed the game and got what I wanted out of it. I knew I was never going to be serious at it. I was not big enough or skilled enough but I could play a reasonable game at most levels most of the time. I was good enough to make the Second XV at St Bernards College for about half a season in my fifth form year, an achievement in a school where rugby was really the only winter sport and where everyone played it. St Bernards 1st XV actually played in the open grades against other "private" colleges and the top state colleges such as Wellington Boys College or Hutt Valley High School and normal club teams. The 2nd XV played the 1st XV teams from other mostly state colleges and other 2nd XVs from the other top schools.

When Dad was drinking violence was never far below the surface in our family. Mum tried to knife Dad when I was about ten or eleven. He had come home late from the pub and she had wanted the car to take me to my grandmother's. Things deteriorated quickly with Mum picking up the family carving knife and trying to stab Dad in front of us all. She very nearly succeeded. My Uncle Jack was present and he saved Mum from a hiding, telling her to go to Nana's with us while he talked to Dad.

I have never, ever laid a finger on a woman I love in anger and I never will. My brother Mark tells me the same. We both grew into men who could look after ourselves very well in a fight but would never hit a woman.

For a short period when I was about twelve or so Mum's drinking increased, probably due to the death of my grandmother Josie who she was very close to. This usually resulted in more dramas at home. Dad contacted the Child Welfare Department one particularly rugged Sunday afternoon and drunkenly asked them to come and take us kids into care. I heard this but did not tell the other kids as I did not want to upset them. Nothing came of this. I think the Child Welfare Officer visited the following week and Mum was able to reassure them that all was well. Mum reduced her drinking dramatically after this, stopping completely within a few years.

Dad eventually pissed off out of our lives when I was twenty eight, leaving mum for another woman. We all continued to make contact with him and tried to have a normal life with him but we were always walking on eggshells around him. He was, initially, a lot happier in his new situation but this relationship also had its issues as time went by. Dad's last years were not that happy either.

I said at his funeral that he was a man of his time. To some extent I think I was right. Domestic violence was not uncommon in Naenae in those days. A lot of men were distant to their children. They did drink a lot. They worked very long hours. They had, most of them, grown up in a depression and then fought a war. Most were likely suffering from some form of Post-Traumatic Stress Disorder but this was not acknowledged in those days.

I am generalising as I know a lot of men who went to war, grew up in the depression, worked hard and were distant to their kids but they were good dads for their time. They did not drink themselves into homicidal rages or beat the people who love them.

Chapter 5

Mum

I should talk about my Mum, Mary Kathleen Knox. She was born in Blenheim when my grandmother, Josie went back to her mother in what seemed to be one of many separations from my grandfather Alf. Josie's parents were Michael Hennessey and Mary Moriarty and they lived in Dunbeath Street, Blenheim. Michael was a barber with his own business. Apparently he was a bit of a scamp and a very handy wordsmith.

Looking at Papers Past I found he features a lot in the advertising columns of the late 19th and early 20th century for the Marlborough Express. He is also in the Court pages a bit as well for civil and criminal matters. He seems to be a natural poet and loved his drink, resulting in some humourous ditties and also some court appearances for drunkenness, fighting, and general misbehavior. Poor Great Grandmother Mary, having to put up with him. He does sound a character though.

Research shows that he was in the British Army in Mauritius at some stage before coming to New Zealand. He would have been too young for the fighting in the land wars so must have come to New Zealand after leaving the Army. He was described as a Sergeant Major and may have been in the Royal Artillery. Coming from Youghal in County Cork, Ireland, he married Mary Moriarty in Blenheim on 8 October 1878, Mary being the second daughter of Mr M C Moriarty, County Kerry, Ireland. Michael died in 1913 with Great Grandmother Mary living a further thirty years in peace. He would have been a character to live with.

As a chap who was no stranger to the long arm of the law I often wonder what he would have thought of quite a few of his descendants becoming Police. He would probably roll in his grave the old codger. I would have loved to have known him.

Nana was the youngest of a large tribe of kids. Her brother Charles died of illness at Gallipoli in 1915 and was buried at sea. His name is apparently with the Aussies at Lone Pine Cemetery. It is also on the war memorial in Blenheim.

Nana worked on the railways in Waterloo to make ends meet. She built a three bed-roomed house at 61 Cudby Street, Waterloo with the original house on the site being pushed back to the end of the section, used by family and then rented out to boarders in later years. The main house has been greatly modernized in recent times but still looks the same from the outside as when Nana lived there. She would be pleased to know that it is now worth many hundreds of thousands of dollars. I recall her telling me that she built if for 850 pounds – about $1700.00 in the 1930s. The latest market price paid was in the vicinity of $750,000

At some stage, when Mum was very small, the family farmed land where Naenae Park is now. Mum recalls nearly drowning in the creek there. I went to school at St Bernadettes, on the edge of the park and used to play in the same creek when I was small. Life seemed pretty hard for the Knoxs back then with Grandad Alf not able to hold down regular paid work due to drinking and ill health.

Mum broke her arm when she was about twelve and never went

back to school, staying at home to look after the younger kids while Nana worked.

Mum's father Alf, my grandfather, was born in Wellington to William Thomas Knox and Lillian Monks, one of nine children. William's father and mother, Henry Knox and Mary Jane Burke, a widow, nee Joyce, arrived in Dunedin about 1874, Mary being from Ireland and Henry from England but earlier Knox generations were from Ireland. As an aside the Earl of Ranfurly is a Knox and there apparently is a family connection. A Lord Ranfurly was Governor-General of New Zealand in the early 20th century and donated the Ranfurly Shield to the New Zealand Rugby Football Union. There is no record of him catching up with his New Zealand cousins. The jury is still out on the family connection but never let the truth get in the way of a good yarn I always say.

Within a short time of Henry and Mary arriving in Dunedin they moved to Wellington. This was due to religious differences between Henry and Mary, Catholics, and Henry's Knox cousins already in Dunedin who were Protestant. The cousins caused the couple some disquiet on St Patricks Day every year, visiting them with the Orange flags and banners and upsetting the neighbours. This move split the family for two generations. Henry and Mary left Dunedin with no forwarding address hoping to cut themselves off from the Dunedin Knox family.

Alf met Josephine Mary Hennessey in Otaki where he was working as a farm labourer after the First World War. Josephine was staying with her older brother who owned a barbershop in Otaki. They married and had six children, Mum being the third born. The marriage was not a happy one despite the large brood and ended in separation about the time of the Second World War starting in 1939.

I only ever met Alf twice before he died, the last time when he was in the Salvation Army home on the corner of Bloomfield Terrace and Laings Road in Lower Hutt, later the Te Omanga Hospice. I was about twelve and Mum took me to see him in my school uniform as I was named after him and she wanted me to see him before he passed away. Robert is his middle name. I remember him being a lovely gentle quiet man, a fact verified by other older cousins who had met him. Mum described him as a book lover and not a very well man from younger days.

I did some research on Alf at the Archives in Wellington and found that he was discharged medically unfit from the Army in about 1941. I had heard from Mum that he served in both World Wars and the issues seem to be stress related. I also heard that he suffered a severe head injury in a flying accident at Wellington airport at the start of the war. There was nothing in his military records about this though. I do not think he left New Zealand in either war but I believe that he served as a guard on Somes Island in Wellington Harbour looking after German and Italian aliens imprisoned for the duration of the wars.

Mum loved her Dad but I think he found work too hard due to health issues. This resulted in severe hardship for Mum's family and Nana having to work as a railway cleaner at Waterloo railway station. I never had the chance to get to know Alf at all really, he died not long after me seeing him at the Salvation Army home. He is buried at Taita Cemetery about thirteen rows up the hill from Nana.

Mum was a land girl in the Wairarapa during the war as well as working at Ford motor company in Gracefield. During the war Ford was converted into an ammunition factory. She always told us of waiting for the Japanese to come into the harbour and shell the factory that was, in those days, on the foreshore. A lot of reclamation has taken place since.

Mum recalled with fondness the US Marines who came to NZ during the war and talked emotionally about a young marine who was her friend. He died in the islands, probably Tarawa, when the Americans began their island-hopping clean-up of the Japs in the Pacific.

Mum's last job before "domestic bliss" was as a buyer for Briscoe Mills, an importing company on Wellington. This resulted in her buying a large amount of expensive crystal and china, some of which has survived to today in the family.

Mum was twenty nine when she had me and, I think, had spent most of her time at home. She had had the odd friendship before she met Dad.

My mother was sweetness itself. She suffered a lot of stress when we were small, mainly due to Dad. Luckily all of us have inherited my mother's nature and her love of independence and privacy. Frankly my mother did not have an easy life at all due to family worries. She spent her last years living with my sister Sarah and her children which did give her some peace at last.

Mum died in her 88th year in a rest home near Sarah's place in Paraparaumu. She had lived with Sarah and her family for quite a few years until a few months before her death when it was not possible for Sarah to keep looking after Mum, whose health was deteriorating.

When we knew Mum was dying I arranged for the local parish priest, Michael McCabe, an old class mate from St Bernadettes and St Bernards, to give Mum extreme unction. Mum recognised Mike and it pleased her that a man she knew as a boy was now the priest blessing her. After Mum passed Mike held a requiem mass for Mum at Our Lady of Kapiti church in Paraparaumu.

Chapter 6

Growing up in Naenae

Growing up in Naenae in the 1950s and 1960s was a fairly healthy time. We had the Olympic Pool which just about all the kids used in summer and I also spent a lot of time in the hills surrounding Naenae doing kids' stuff, camping, using bush swings, playing war games with my mates, collecting and selling blackberries, going to the pictures every Saturday at 2.00 p.m. at the Regent picture theatre. Naenae was a very safe place in those days and Mum did not mind me leaving after breakfast and not coming home until dinner time or when my stomach bought me home. I had cousins up the road, the McHughs, and plenty of other boys around my own age to kick around with.

We often biked to Wellington Harbour and fished off Petone Wharf, the docks in Wellington or around the Eastbourne and Muritai coasts off the rocks. We never seemed to catch many fish but always had a great time, cycling home at the end of the day absolutely worn out.

I lived in three homes while growing up in Naenae, a small cottage Dad and his first wife owned at 37 Toomath Street, a three-bedroomed home on a hill at 39 Kowhai Street and lastly, a four bedroomed home at 98 Kowhai Street, the houses getting bigger as the tribe grew. The homes in Kowhai Street were both new when we shifted in and Dad broke the sections in himself. He and Mum liked gardening so outside the houses always looked good.

We never had a car until I was about 8. Mum and Dad used to walk everywhere, with Dad cycling to work in Gracefield. This was not unusual for the times. The cars that were around in Naenae were all mostly very old as times were a bit tight after the war for working people. We also never had a phone in the house until about 1958. Mum used to have to visit a neighbour or walk to a phone box to ring anyone. If Mum had to go shopping I was usually kept home from school to push the pram for Sarah who was a baby at the time as Mum pushed Gail and Lynne in a twin pushchair from home to the Naenae shops. She would get the groceries, pay for them and the shop would deliver them later in the day. Everyone did this. In those days we also had a mobile grocery shop, a mobile fruit shop, our bread and milk delivered daily and even a fish-monger who would call on his rounds. Many of the Naenae shops had not been built and the closest decent shops were in Lower Hutt, 3 miles away. We had a very good bus service run by the Railways, which we used to go to the Hutt or later, to school. We mostly walked or rode our bikes everywhere. We did not know any different. There were no issues with obesity, child or adult, in those days.

Due to the age gap between me and my sisters Lynne and Sarah, five years, I was at a loose end a lot of the time and basically did not fit in with the rest of the family. Gail was away from home periodically to start with and then full time from the age of seven.

This resulted in me spending most of my weekends from the age of about eight or nine until I was about eleven staying with my Nana Josephine Knox at 61 Cudby Street in Waterloo. Nana loved me to bits and looked after me well. My mother grew up in this house and so it has always been special to me.

Nana had thrown my grandfather Alf out years before because of his drinking but she never divorced him and never looked elsewhere. Nana died when I was eleven in my bed in our home in Naenae. She had been ill for some time and Mum bought her home to care for her. Nana – Josephine Mary Knox, (nee Hennessey) was a huge influence on my life. As it was, from the age of about eight onwards I spent most of my spare time at weekends with Nana and being immersed in a very strong Irish environment. All Nana's friends were Irish or of Irish descent. They were working people, honest in their own way but always up for an opportunity if one came their way. Horse racing was a very popular pastime. There was drinking but not by Nana. She liked a beer once a week but that was all.

Mick and Min Boyle were an older Irish couple who lived with Nana for years in the old bach at the back of the section at 61 Cudby Street, Waterloo. They looked after Nana and she provided them with a home base. They liked their wee tipple and were delightful people. Both worked in factories in Gracefield or Petone, Min working at WD and HO Wills tobacco factory. She always had bags of smokes she had pinched. Mick always sent me to the shop for the paper, giving me a half crown for the effort. The paper only cost fourpence! Good deal. I never told Nana as she would have made me give the change back to Mick. Nana was a straight shooter, said what she believed and did not suffer fools

Dad was wary of Nana so he behaved himself when she was alive. Dad's behaviour deteriorated after her death. He became more abusive towards Mum, assaulting her regularly when drunk. He was an evil bastard when he had been drinking and you learnt to keep out of his way. When I was about fourteen I was big enough to stand up to him. I was only a little guy and I caught Dad giving Mum a bit of swish in their bedroom one night. I stopped him and, as far as I know from that day until I left home three years later he never touched Mum again.

I only found out recently from Sarah and Mark that after I left home to join the Police in 1970 Dad began smacking Mum around again. I asked them why they did not tell me and they said they were scared I would do something that would get me fired from the Police. Poor kids, they were only young when I left home. Mum would never mention anything to me either.

Home was full of tension in those days. As I have said Mum took to drinking for a short while but gave it away completely within a short time. She never touched alcohol again that I know of.

My memories of my life at home really from about the age of five contain images of Mum getting assaulted by Dad when he was pissed. Mum could handle Dad when he was sober though. Mum bought my sister Gail and I dressing gowns when I was about five. That night when Dad saw them he punched Mum at the table. I have no idea why.

I lost a lot of school time staying home to look after Mum and the little kids after Dad's outbursts. When I was eleven I was in a composite Form 1 and 2 class for bright little buggers at St Bernards Primary. I was absent for 48% of the school time. The teacher, Reg Wilton, made me do the percentage one day. This was a particularly fraught period in our home. I also do not remember much about Fourth Form either, another messy time looking after Mum and my siblings. I managed to bottom Fourth Form for some reason – not really surprising.

When I was in Form 2 my class used to take the train to Naenae and go to woodwork at Naenae School every Monday morning. On Mum's birthday that year Mum and Dad had an argument which ended in Dad hitting Mum in the face, cutting her head. This on her birthday. He had also not bought her a present. The next day, Monday, I went to woodwork as usual but when we got to Naenae I left my mates and went to Woolworths in Naenae to buy Mum a birthday present, a handkerchief, which I took home to her. She cried when I turned up at home in the middle of the day with the present. I then caught up with my schoolmates at the railway station and went back to school.

This sort of carry on probably was the reason I spent two years in Fifth Form, failing School Certificate abysmally in my first year. I just had too much stuff going on at home and was too anxious most of the time about what was going to happen next with Dad in my early teens to be able to put the time in to the work. I liked my subjects but the stream I was in at school meant that I had to study French, Latin, Physics, Chemistry as well as English and Mathematics. I really had to work at one or two of these subjects to do well but somehow I completely got it all wrong and went back for a second go, cleaning up completely with surprisingly good marks. I then left school for the Police and left home at seventeen.

In the 1960s if you missed School Certificate or University Entrance you stayed behind to do it again or you left school. Kids learned how to deal with failure back then. Most did make the grade eventually but many left school without any qualifications at all.

Chapter 7

Primary School and Church Life

I began school at St Bernadettes Convent in Naenae, being taught by the Sisters of Mercy, a gentle breed who tried to spare the rod and spoil the child. This did not work with the types of kids they had to teach. As a result the odd sound beating was handed out. I received more than my share of these for various sins such as not learning the answers to my catechism questions, a nightly chore, or being disruptive, usually as a result of being picked on, well that's my story.

The best beating I can recall was when my good friend Peter Warbrick and I had a small difference of opinion in Standard 1 over where we sat in class. We were attempting to negotiate a few small points when the Sister walked in. We had moved our negotiations from the top of the desk to the floor of the classroom when she laid into both of us with a leather strap. She must have been having a bad day. By the time she finished neither Peter nor I could walk very well. I remember my mother seeing the bruises on my legs and not being much impressed. Mum was not slow in coming forward and explaining her thoughts to people. She visited the school the next day and sorted the nun out.

Despite the above I remember my time at St Bernadettes as very happy. It was a huge school as Naenae was full of Irish and Italian Catholics, being a "working class" suburb. It was overall a Pakeha school in a Pakeha town. The Warbricks, Weitzels and the Churchwards being the only Maori families I remember from that time at school.

There was still a bit of sectarian nonsense present in the fifties. We Catholic kids had to pass at least one state school to get home from school. This sometimes resulted in stone-throwing competitions (fights) between the "Proddie Dogs" and we more enlightened "Catholic Dogs". I do not remember this as being a "fun time". Some of these encounters were pretty traumatic with blood being shed on occasions. I recall individuals from this time who I would still gladly like to meet in a dark alley. I am sure the feelings would be mutual.

When I was small I had to walk the length of Naenae Road to Kowhai Street, passing the kids from Rata Street School each way. The senior girls and boys in our school usually took us wee ones home. This was good for a couple of years but from about the age of seven I decided to fend for myself. I usually managed at least one ruck a week, losing the first few but gradually getting the upper hand until either I was left alone or I made friends with the kids involved.

The worst thing about this was that the Catholic Church was not allowed to establish dental clinics at its own schools. We had to go to the nearest state school to visit the dental clinic. This was an interesting experience if one arrived at the school while class was not in session. We also wore a school uniform, standing out somewhat from the other kids. Needless to say the dental health of a lot of Catholic boys of my age who grew up in that area was not the best until College years. I usually found a reason to play in the creek in Naenae park rather than bother with the dentist, going back to school when I thought I had been away long enough.

From eighteen months old I have been cursed with asthma. As a result I spent a lot of time away from school in my younger days. Despite this I did reasonably well academically. The asthma disappeared in my teens, only to re-emerge in my thirties. I was always in the top stream right through but struggled with the motivation of the whole thing. I guess, looking back, I was a frustrating kid to teach as I could certainly have done a lot better than I did. Most teachers, after spending the first term of any year encouraging me, promptly gave up and moved on to more deserving cases. This suited me anyway. My school reports from that time all have that familiar theme – could do better if only he would try.

When I was eight I was hospitalised with asthma. It nearly killed me. I, obviously, recovered. I was sent to Otaki Health Camp for six weeks with other Naenae children. The health camps are set up for under-nourished, sickly children and are great at getting kids back on their feet. I mostly hated my time at the camp, running up against the matron for licking my plate in the dining room. Bad manners! I also got in trouble for smacking another kid with the swing. It was an accident but he was a very sick kid and it looked like I had done it on purpose. Oh well, another 500 lines. – "I must be nice to …"

I missed my home, my parents and family and my own schoolmates. In fact I spent most of my leisure time during the six weeks I was in the health camp doing lines for various sins. What I did not realise at the time was that the matron and my dear old Dad had had a ding dong argument when he dropped me and four other kids off at the health camp bus in Wellington. Of the families whose kids came from our neighbourhood we were the only family to have a car so Dad had kindly offered to take us all in to the bus, the Bell kids from over the road and two Ferrier girls from the house behind ours and me. He had bought bags of apples and some lollipops for us to eat on the journey to Otaki but the matron had confiscated them, saying he had no right to do this. Dad complained to the Health department about the matron's nasty behaviour and so I guess she took this out on me, telling me one day in one of my many visits to her office for a telling off that I was "a dirty rotten cow just like your father". This surprised me but I was only eight, turning nine while I was in the camp and did not think anything of it as she was always shouting at me or any other of the more lively kids in my group. Dad's complaint must have been the last straw for this woman as she was replaced while I was in the camp.

We had to go to school at the camp and the lessons bored me witless as I had already covered all the work at St Bernadette's. One incident did mark me while in the tender care of the state. The "nurses" had a practice of dragging misbehaving little boys down to the girls' dormitory and taking the boys' pants down and smacking them on the bare bottom in front of the little girls. This really upset the little girls apart from absolutely traumatising the little boy concerned. They tried this with me and I fought tooth and nail. I actually cannot remember if they succeeded in beating me in front of the girls but they must have as the girls were very upset the next day, saying how I was crying and asking them to stop. To this day I hope those "nurses" rot in hell for what they did to us sick little kids.

One of my friends at that time, Kevin Bell, went with me to the camp. His sister Jenny came also. They were not thriving that well at the time. Kevin and I were really good little mates who, at that time, also went to school together. Kevin and I planned to run away and go home but we made the mistake of writing to our parents about this. Somehow the matron found out and we both got into trouble again. I do not think the letters were even posted.

When we became teenagers Kevin turned to a life of crime, becoming a bit of a thug and petty criminal for a while. He eventually married and settled down, becoming a very responsible senior employee of the Lower Hutt City Council.

When I was a cop in the Hutt Kevin and I caught up one day for a chat as grown men. Ding was pleased for me that my life was going well. I asked him how he was and he said great now, but he could have done without going to the Health Camp in 1961. I remembered then the beatings he received as he was a lot tougher than me and did not mind standing up to people. We had a bit of a moment and went our separate ways. We had little in common by then other than growing up over the road from each other as kids. Ding died last year. He would only have been sixty five. I often wondered if the way he was treated at the Health Camp contributed towards his problems later in his teens and young adult life. I know it really affected me. I was always an anxious kid apparently but now I also became easily irritated and a bit quick-tempered, a fault I still try to control to this day. Upon coming home from the camp I tended to get into fights a lot more than I had previously. Looking back I think I was very angry about the way some of us were treated at the camp.

I spent months away from School due to Asthma. In those days there was not the medication available so when an attack happened I just spent time at home until my breathing improved. There was medication but this was hit and miss at times. The absence from school probably did affect my schooling but I seemed to do well enough until College years. A positive side effect was the fact that I read a lot of books while recovering, a passion I still enjoy today.

One of my teachers, Sister Mary Jacinta, used to send work home for me, usually using Patrick Tohill, a classmate who lived around the corner. I recently thanked Pat for this at a 3rd form reunion we were at in the Hutt in August 2017. I do not think he remembered it but I was pleased at the time.

I seemed to have been a handful in my younger primary school years. Most teachers just strapped or caned me but one or two seemed to know what to do to keep me occupied and quiet. I guess nowadays I would have been given a label by a school social worker or psychologist but in those days they just belted you if you were a gobby, stroppy, loud and bored kid.

Mum always liked us kids joining clubs and groups. When I was about nine she thought it would be a good idea for me to join the St John Boscoe Scouts cub pack. This was a Catholic scout group and most of my mates from St Bernadettes were members. The scout hall was in the grounds of St Thomas's convent in Naenae Road, Lower Hutt. The convent building was built as Balgownie House by John Duthie, a politician and businessman, in 1903. It is still there, a beautiful old mansion. After Duthie died the Sisters of Mercy order bought the house and used it as a boys' home for many years. In my time the sisters still lived there and travelled daily to St Bernadettes to teach us. It is now privately owned and seems to have been refurbished.

I enjoyed being a cub but the old asthma kept me away from quite a few of the activities. The cub-master was Mr Isherwood, the father of Neville, a mate of mine from school. He was a really good bloke and was helped by a selection of other fathers to manage quite a large cub pack.

When I turned eleven I became a scout with all my other mates. I really liked scouting and got right into it. The camps were fun as I had always liked the bush and camping. However it all turned to custard.

One night the phone rang at home – "Hello Mrs Rattenbury. Ron Watts, scoutmaster of St John Boscoe here. We have had a meeting and I am ringing you to tell you that following some issues we believe that Robert would be better not coming to Scouts anymore."

Mum was gob-smacked, looking at me with that look I knew so well, I am for it. She asked Mr Watts why. The scout troop had just come back from a ten day camp at Martinborough where we were doing work for merit badges. I had to take my asthma medication with me and this caused the scoutmasters some worry although I was fine the whole time. On the last day I was helping to pack up our patrol's tent and was, as usual, skylarking. The Troop Leader, a fifteen year named Terry, grabbed me by my scarf and woggle and began shaking me, telling me to behave myself. I punched him on the chest as hard as I could, a normal reaction from me at that time when I was scared or angry. Instead of giving me the bash I then expected as he was a lot bigger than me, he went away and apparently bleated to the scout masters. I did not think anything more of it and carried on packing the gear.

It was decided that I was too much trouble for the troop and I had to hand in my woggle. When I told Mum what had happened she asked if I would like her to talk to Mr Watts again. I declined as I knew it would be only a matter of time before something else happened. He did not really want me in the troop as I was just a problem he did not need. The sad thing was that I knew this as a young kid. Nice to know you are not welcome.

One of the useful skills I learned as a scout, other than the normal skills of bush-craft, was map-reading. For some reason this skill remained with me and became useful when I was a Police cadet doing Search and Rescue training in the Tararuas in 1971 and then again as an instructor on the Armed Offenders Squad Qualifying Courses I helped with from 1989 to 1991. Many Police who aspire to work on the Armed Offender Squad have good bush skills anyway but some do not. The ability to read maps and to plot routes is a vital skill for AOS staff to possess, especially staff in the rural regions of New Zealand as a lot of the squad's work is undertaken in bush conditions.

My devotion to the Catholic Church was absolute until I left College. I always had very good teachers, especially in College. I have remained and will remain a Catholic, occasionally practising, but with a healthy disdain for some of the ways of the Church. The Church, together with my grandmother Josie and my mother, has given me the values that I try to live by. I used to attend Mass at least weekly, sometimes twice-weekly.

I seemed to miss the cut for the altar boy roster probably due to my generally disruptive behaviour. I was not a pretty little kid either and was a bit "rough" so to speak. This did not worry me after hearing from my school mates about them having to get up for 6.30 a.m. Mass in all weathers, sometimes several times a week. My brother Mark made the cut, something he likes to remind me of every time we catch up. He is prettier than me but is now bald and I am not.

I did not realise it until I became an adult but my parents instilled in all of us a tolerance for people of different religions, lifestyles and races. Being Maori Dad had a lot of Maori mates and I grew up not even thinking about racial differences. Criticism of gay people was not put up with by either of my parents and we were encouraged to play with kids from other religions unlike some Catholic families.

I have identified as part Maori all of my adult life and am quick to point this out to anyone giving Maori a hard time. I am white but I can trace my whakapapa back to the Tokomaru canoe. I am very comfortable in the company of Maori in a Maori environment as well as with Pakeha. I feel more accepted for myself with Maori, this especially so when I was younger. I am more relaxed in the company of Maori or Polynesian mates for some reason I cannot explain. I can speak te reo a bit but certainly am not fluent. I can move comfortably in both worlds and, believe me, they are very different worlds. Pakeha could learn a lot from Maori if they were generally more interested.

Being a cop of Maori descent did not make any difference to me other than when dealing with the death of Maori. I knew from my own upbringing and from talking to my mates what was required for whanau dealing with the passing of a loved one.

Chapter 8

Secondary School

I started at St Bernard's College for boys in Waterloo, Lower Hutt in standard four as a ten-year-old. In those days all the teachers, with the exception of two, were Marist Brothers. We thought we were pretty tough but the Brothers were Hard Men. The cane was never far from hand and endowed with generous ferocity. They taught us academic subjects, coached us in Rugby, Athletics and Cricket, acted as our mentors and, despite the cane, taught us a sense of social justice that, I believe, never leaves a person. Sport was compulsory. To get out of sport you had to have a note from your parents, thereby inviting the eternal condemnation of your peers as being "one of those". I continued to do well academically, but making sure never to do too well as this resulted in more challenging home-work and the requirement to become involved in extra-curricular activities at school. I remained in the top stream of school until I left at seventeen.

The Marist Brothers were a mixed bag, ranging from sensitive academic types who found teaching a bunch of working class Catholic boys a challenge, to down-to-earth teachers who also excelled on the sports field. I can recall brilliant teachers from that time, Brother Baptist, the published author of physics texts under his own name, Brother Roger, hard man, mercurial, brilliant music and English teacher, a dabbler in the languages, and a brilliant coach at athletics and rugby. Brother Cyprian, the Headmaster. A quiet scholarly man, not in the best of health, but an approachable and understanding man. Brother Ambrose, a

Chemistry teacher par excellence who also tried to bash the mysteries of Latin, Algebra, Geography and French into our thick heads. A slight, academic man who was brilliant as the First XV Coach. Brother Majella, another specialised in athletics coaching and who, in my third form year made me run the 440 yards in 63s because he convinced me that I was able to. There may have been something wrong with his stopwatch. Brother Quentin who put up with me in the 2nd XV and tried to make me the Rugby Winger I was not. I often wonder about these wonderful, talented men and what became of them.

They were, without exception, devout holy men of strong character whose only ambition in life was to mould the lives of Catholic boys to become outstanding members of their communities. I sometimes wish I had valued their counsel more than I did. I was still, in my early teens, the gobby, stroppy and noisy kid I had always been. It was due to my mother that I received the sound education I did. Right or wrong I was going to be taught by the Marist Brothers, as my Uncle Bill, Mum's youngest brother, had been a foundation pupil of the school, going on to join the Police. He was the apple of my Mum's eye and she wanted me to turn out like him. I guess I did – to a degree.

I left school at seventeen. I remember being berated by Brother Roger for leaving to enter the Police, a move he regarded as a waste of time and talent. In my last year at school there were fifty six boys in my form class. Out of that class twenty four went on straight from college to obtain university degrees, three became senior Police Officers and three trained for the Marist order to become brothers. Many, including myself, have undertaken subsequent university studies. Several went into the business world and have become successes in their fields. The

Marist Brothers achieved miracles with a lot of us. I laugh when I hear teachers today moan about the teacher/pupil ratio.

As mentioned above I did spend quite a bit of time away from school, as much as possible actually, and did not really settle downto college life until my last year or so at school. Schools in the 50's and 60's still caned first and asked questions later. I was, for some reason, constantly caned by certain teachers. I do not think I was picked on, because plenty of my mates got it as well. I suppose a lot of my "wagging" was, apart from asthma, usually related to the fact that I could not bother doing homework, especially in the lower forms, and I knew that I would get caned for this omission, so chose not to attend.

I also spent a lot of time on detention due to being late for class, not doing homework etc. I was never in any danger of being asked to be a prefect although I would dearly and secretly have loved to have been one.

People nowadays always assume that I was an altar boy at my grandmother's requiem mass. I wasn't but two cousins I went to school with, Kevin and Chris Knox, were. I am glad they have memories of me like that however wrong they were.

I needed to get away from Naenae. I had school friends who I had known since the age of five and who were and are good, achieving, successful and intelligent guys. However I had "mates" away from school who were always on the fringes of the law or actually committing crime.

This was brought home to me in late 1973 when I was stationed as a Constable in Masterton. I was sent to a reported domestic dispute at a flat in Worksop Road. In those days we mostly worked alone due to lack of staff so I was, as usual, very careful about approaching the address. I knocked on the front door to the address and a young woman answered. She looked vaguely familiar. Behind her was her partner. They seemed a really nice young couple. Upon seeing me she said "Robert Rattenbury – what are you doing in that uniform, you were a bit of a shit as a kid. How did you get into the Police?"

I was taken aback and then recognised the young woman from Naenae. She grew up down the road from our home. I knew her by sight and name but had never spoken to her. Her Dad was the groundsman and caretaker at Rata Street School. Amazing what people think of you when they do not know you.

We had a good chat and a laugh and I think she was impressed that I had made the break from what, in her mind, was a risky life. There was no domestic dispute. I seem to remember that they had been having some hi-jinks and making a bit of noise, upsetting the neighbours.

Naenae had more than its share of criminals and growing up there you made a choice, join the crowd and get involved in the thieving, assaults and burglary, change the crowd you are in or leave. When I was about fourteen to fifteen I did get mixed up with a bunch of unsavoury characters but had enough brains not to get involved in their dirty deals. This association ended when one of them left home and the district after his father died. He was a really good mate of mine but got into trouble for stealing from his employer after leaving school at fifteen. The bad boys were schoolmates of his from Naenae College and I just found myself tagging along in the group. I really was not tough enough and too honest for these clowns anyway. I was wagging school a lot at this time as well. My parents were going through another bad patch also so I got away with a lot more than I should have.

For some reason that I cannot recall now I decided to pull my socks up. I kept away from the shitheads and started concentrating on school. I joined my church youth group, the Legion of Mary and also the Catholic Youth Movement. These two groups succeeded in using up a lot of my spare time helping old age parishioners with lawn-mowing etc. It also meant that I socialised mainly with my school mates and girls from Sacred Heart College, a much healthier association. This continued until I left school. I was aware then that if I wanted to join the Police I really needed to be careful who I associated with and I also needed good exam results to get into the Cadets.

The result was that my performance at school improved dramatically in my last year at school and that I attended more regularly. I was getting really pissed off with breaking up the arguments at home and dealing with Dad's drinking and his bloody mind games. Being the eldest it always fell to me to sort him out and stop him knocking Mum around when he was drunk, which was fine as Mark, the next boy, was only eight. I did not have to do much as Dad had had his wake-up call when I was fourteen so he knew not to tangle with me. But is this any way to live?

Overall I really enjoyed my time at St Bernards. The fact that I missed a lot of school and was a bit naughty quite a bit of the time had nothing to do with the school and all to do with stuff away from school. I am the better person for having had the opportunity to attend a school with such a special character. I believe that the school instilled strong character in most of the boys, helping most of us make a very good fist of our lives.

In early 2017 I was talking to a couple of my lifelong class mates on Facebook, Terry Jordan and Pat Quin, when I proposed the idea of having a reunion of our 1966 third form class. I had lost touch with nearly all my old classmates but I have many great memories of them all. I thought it would be nice to see if a few of us could get together once more before we all shuffled off this mortal coil.

Terry offered to help by way of being the man on the ground in Lower Hutt where he still lives. He would arrange the venues and catering and I would find the guys. We planned to have the reunion in Lower Hutt in August 2017. I had contact with a few more schoolmates on Facebook and they were all very keen, providing names and locations. One provided a list of our three form 3 classes from 1966.

For the next few months I tracked down, with the assistance of other classmates, our local library and other sources, some 80 odd classmates from 1966. The total class that year was around one hundred and twenty boys so this was not bad after over fifty years. Of the eighty guys I found eight had passed away. Of the remaining seventy two odd guys a total of close to sixty made it to the reunion, either for one night or for both nights of the gathering. Some were overseas and could not get home, some were heading overseas on planned trips and could not make it and one or two were too sick to attend. Only two guys point blank refused to come. About another six just did not reply to my letters or e-mails. This was a great response.

In late August 2017, one weekend, we held the reunion over two nights in the Angus Inn in Lower Hutt, about half a mile down Waterloo Road from our old school. Several of us visited the school on the Saturday afternoon and were shown around by the

Sports Master. It is a lot flasher nowadays than I remember.

Talking to all the guys I was amazed at how well everybody seemed to have done in their lives. After an initial nervous start we were all back to where we had been as spotty teenage boys, giving each other a hard time in a friendly way and remembering deeds and misdeeds from our teenage years best forgotten. One or two were still arguing about things that happened fifty years ago. What impressed me the most is that I had forgotten how good these guys were and are. They were still the friendly, considerate chaps I remember from school. The reunion was basically a talkfest. It felt really good to make contact again with many guys I had known since we were five year olds in Naenae.

Chapter 9

A New Life - Why the Police

You may notice from the following stories that they are all about the "working" end of the Police, the Constables, Detectives and NCOs. This does not mean that I do not respect the many very fine Commissioned Officers I served with and worked for over the years, it just means that these stories are about the guys and girls at the coalface and the daily trials and tribulations of the "working copper", someone I was very proud to call myself.

Most people in my stories did not reach high rank or have to deal with the very heavy responsibility that goes with those positions. Some did, but they all started as "working coppers" and were mostly better leaders and managers for it.

Some not so but the system seemed to solve this. Some people join the Police to simply climb the ranks as soon as possible. They have no real interest in being cops, dealing with crime etc. They do the bare minimum to get by and are not usually respected much by their peers. However they can pass exams and, in the old days, if you kept your nose clean, passed your exams and managed to never have many complaints from the public you could guarantee an easy ride up the ranks. This resulted in quite a few knob-heads managing to become Inspectors or above before they were found out and sent on "gardening leave". These people, with a bit of luck, will find themselves a cushy number in National Headquarters and hope never to see the sharp end of Policing again until they, if they really brown-nose with the right people, find themselves given a

District as a Superintendent or retire on a very healthy pension.

This was clearly evident during the Springbok Tour in 1981. I was stationed in Wellington and was amazed at the number of Inspectors and Chief Inspectors who were based in Wellington but unknown to me. They had been dragged out of Headquarters and told to run "Groups" of street-hardened Constables, Detectives and NCOs in riot situations. Some made a good fist of it and then sank thankfully back into Headquarters after the Tour but quite a few were hopeless, losing the plot, making very bad decisions and not being able to handle these being questioned by their Senior Sergeants or Sergeants. Later I talk about one incident where the Inspector just got in his car and left the scene of a very serious incident because he could not handle it.

Some of these people actually get through to very high positions in the Police on the good work of their staff, taking credit for this. Once they get to these positions they then do quite a bit of damage to the Police wherever they happen to be before getting the boot. Some even mange to retire which is amazing. They spend a career being despised or laughed at by their staff and their peers. They must have hides like a rhinoceros.

On the other hand many fine men and women become Commissioned Officers and lead by example, much respected and admired by everyone. Thankfully these greatly outnumber the knob-heads.

I reached the exalted and heady position of Senior Sergeant, in my day the actual rank that ran most UB groups and CIB offices.

Even at this position I was beginning to be sidelined away from the actual role of policing I joined to do. There were and are very good reasons for this. Why have Sergeants if you have Senior Sergeants butting in all the time? Also someone had to interpret some of the orders and instructions from above to make them palatable and workable for the troops.

The Senior Sergeant was also the friend of the working copper at the daily "prayer" or management meetings in the large stations I worked in when some understanding needed to be displayed on occasions by the senior management of the station. Believe me some very frank discussions used to take place in the District Commander's office at times. A Senior Sergeant was always best placed to do this as he or she had to have the finger on the pulse on the ground floor where the Uniform Branch works in most stations or in the CIB office upstairs.

This did not mean that the troops got away with too much, but that any action was leavened with some common sense. Well that was the aim anyway.

I never aspired to high rank in the Police but I certainly admire people who have the courage to give it a go. It is a very lonely path to take and it is not for everyone. Also I would not have had all these stories to tell if I had been side-tracked by too much ambition or if I worried too much about blotting my copybook, silly details I disposed of at a very young age, deciding to concentrate on my family and out of work activities.

The most admirable trait of the New Zealand Police Officer apart from the quality of honesty required, is that he or she started as a Constable working the streets. No rank is gifted and no position assured at any stage in a good cop's career. The rare times this has not happened have proved abject failures.

In February of 1969, my last year at school at St Bernard's

College in Lower Hutt, I turned up at Wellington Central Police station in my school uniform and asked to see the Recruiting Sergeant. This large, friendly bear of a man met me with a smile and asked me if I was related to Ron Rattenbury. I told him I was Ron's son. He introduced himself to me, Jim Weekes, and told me he had gone to school with Dad in Urenui.

"So you want to be a cop Robert" was the next question. I replied that I was very keen but that I had to finish school first as I was only sixteen. We went to Jim's office and he gave me an IQ test, a memory test and asked me to write some stuff. He then sent me on my way, saying he would be in touch.

About a month later Jim rang me to say that he wanted me to do some medical tests and that the pre-entry written tests had gone very well. I did the medical tests over the following week or so, had an interview with a couple of senior officers in Lower Hutt police station, Mum and Dad also being interviewed. The officers asked Mum and Dad what they thought about me joining the Police. Dad was supportive but Mum bluntly said she did not want me to be a cop as it was too dangerous. I was told in about June 1969 that I had been accepted for the next Police Cadet intake at the Police Training School in Trentham Army Camp in January 1970, but that I had better do well at school in the meantime.

I was sure, from about the age of fourteen or fifteen that I was going to be a cop. My uncle Bill Knox was a cop in Wellington in the 50's and 60's and was a hero to me. He used to turn up at home in Naenae with the Police van on escort to Wi Tako Prison, usually with one or two "guests" in the back, for a cup of tea. He looked good, was full of blarney, and seemed so far above the other men of his age in the area I grew up in. My cousin, Kevin Knox, had joined the Police Cadets while I was at college and, being a St Bernard's Old Boy, came back to the college with the recruiter to talk to us. He managed to catch three from my class, Tim Belcher, John Kelly and I. Tim and I joined the number 14 Percy B Allen Cadet Wing, John joined up in a subsequent Recruit Training Course just after us, topping the course. We all went on to have long careers, all taking promotion with John having reached very high rank.

Having a history of asthma I was worried that this would stop me from entering the Police but I passed the medical examination with flying colours. By this time the asthma was, for all intents and purposes, gone. This happens sometimes as children become teenagers. So all good. With my social history it may have been a different story if the Police also did psychometric tests in those days.

I never really saw myself in an office job or trade and was not interested in university after school, something I got around to doing later in life. The only other option was factory work in Gracefield which held little appeal after spending most of my school holidays working at Winstones Gibraltar Board as a factory hand. I had an interest in helping others but was certainly not saintly enough to consider the Church. I had played sport all my life and did not mind a bit of rough and tumble, so to speak. Policing seemed a good option.

Another Police Officer who had a profound impact on me and my decision to join the Police was Naenae's Constable, Hapeta (Hoppy) Watene Hodges. Hoppy was a legend in his own time in Naenae. Physically a big man he had a tough beat dealing with the legendary "bodgies" in the Naenae/Taita area in the late fities/sixties. Legend has it that he would normally sort most problems out behind the Naenae shops on a man-to-man basis with the trouble-maker. There must have been some truth in the legend as, in later years as a cop in Lower Hutt, I would deal with the same idiots who would constantly quote the times they had been on the receiving end of Hoppy's rehabilitative justice. When Hoppy walked through the Naenae shopping centre it became a very peaceful place to be. Hoppy and I later became good friends. He had a long and distinguished career in the Hutt Valley, eventually retiring to the Wairarapa.

I was still a skinny kid at sixteen and was an inch or two short of the required chest measurements. Jim Weekes signed me up for his "self-defence" classes at the YMCA in Birch Street, Lower Hutt.

During my last year at College, while waiting for January 1970, the start of Cadet Training, I attended his gym to learn the manly art of killing people using nothing but my hands. I think natural growth took care of the chest measurement problem. Jim's tutoring in judo, boxing and other methods of making your opponent's life generally quite miserable certainly gave me further confidence in myself, standing me in good stead in later years as a cop.

Policing does run in families like nursing, building, the law, medicine etc. It has now hit the third generation in my family – my son Luke joined the Police in 2005 after six years Army service, mainly overseas. He is now an instructor at the Police College.

When I joined the Police there were two methods of entry, the recruit system and the cadet system. Recruits aged nineteen to thirty five had to do a three months course at the old Police school in Trentham Army Camp. Cadets aged seventeen to eighteen years and did a nineteen month course at the school.

The Police Cadet system in New Zealand started in 1957, modeled on English examples. The difference being that NZ Cadets graduated as Probationary Constables, whereas English Cadets, at the end of training, had to undergo a Recruit Training Course. The reason for the Cadet system depends on whom you listen to. The Police wanted to capture talented young men (no females underwent cadet training until about 1981 for some reason) direct from College to inculcate in the Police culture with a view to developing strong NCOs and Commissioned Officers. The Leaders of Tomorrow.

Needless to say being a Cadet or ex-Cadet invited a certain amount of derision or antagonism from older serving Police. This still exists in a humourous way today, but how many recruit courses have reunions nowadays. My cadet wing still meets every five years for a reunion, gathering from the four corners of the world.

28th January 1970, eighty two nervous young men with freshly shorn hair gathered in the lounge at Holland House Police Barracks, Wellington to begin their careers in the New Zealand Police. We were all between seventeen and eighteen years of age, "soundly educated", supposedly of above average intelligence and physique, predominantly Pakeha and working/middle class. I was joined by Gary McClure as the only two boys from Naenae. Others from the Hutt Valley were Tim Belcher, Malcolm Bennett, Martyn Wright, Vic Jarvis and Stu Rolph. We were met by the Course Co- Ordinator, Senior Sergeant Ian Forsyth Croxford. An interesting chap! He spent a lot of time shouting and strutting up and down. He certainly established the fact that being a Cadet was not necessarily a passport to future security.

We were all marched onto buses and driven to the Police Store in Newtown to receive uniforms and the famous Navy Blue Beret signifying that we were Police Cadets, a life form somewhere level with a Police Dog's knee. We then set forth out along the new Western Motorway to Trentham Army Camp where the Police Training School was then situated. Upon arrival we were all greeted with a row of tin huts, "temporary" Army accommodation dating back to World War 1. One cadet on my bus took one look, went into the reception office and resigned there and then. Thus began a three month period of getting used to living with others, being away from home for the first time, coping with different ideas on how to do things and putting up with what I still believe to be petty restrictions and attitudes from instructors.

My being made to roll under my bunk in full parade uniform because the instructor found some dust in my cubicle did not help me develop into a competent police officer. A certain amount of "razzing" had to be suffered. This, in a weird way, did help development. As a cop the requirement to handle provocation and abuse is part of the job.

The cadet system was challenging in many ways and a few left within the first year, either by choice or compulsion. Failure to achieve academically resulted in most departures. I gradually came to accept the way of life. At the end of the first term, or three months into the course, I returned home on leave and found I missed Trentham! I also found that I was in the top 20% of the wing academically. This would have to stop. I did not want the instructors taking too much notice of me. I managed over the next fifteen months to wheedle my way into the bottom third of the wing, doing just enough to pass, which rather suited my attitude to social life outside of Trentham – I was still in my home town and most of my social activities were with mates from Naenae and college.

The Cadet day consisted of class room lectures in Police Law and Practice, Arithmetic, English, Sociology, Geography, a daily session of drill, at least one hour of physical training under the gentle care of Senior Sergeant Jimmy Page and study in the evenings. We were also taught to type by Mrs Benge, a long-suffering woman who had been teaching Cadets since 1957. Our Police instructors were experienced Sergeants or Senior Sergeants. Our Education Instructors were a mixed bag of teachers. I personally found some of them wanting compared to the teachers I had had at College. They were not, in my opinion, an inspiring lot. The exceptions to this were John O'Hara and Barry Mason. John was tasked with teaching us sociology and English. John's refined manner and polite way of addressing us was unusual. He seemed to treat us with respect! I think he despaired at trying to teach us though at times. Most of us had at least School Certificate and found the education subjects irksome. John is a great guy and still attends all our reunions.

Once a week there was the "Saturday Morning Test" in law and practice. Failure to achieve a 60% pass in this could result in dismissal. Mostly we achieved the required pass. Those of us who did not lived in fear for the next few days awaiting the call to the Commandant's Office. In the nineteen months at the Training School I think I managed three failed Saturday morning tests. I certainly lifted my act following these events. The School at that time was under the care of Superintendent Ted Hotham, a gentle man who knew Cadets and the behaviour of young people. I believe that his tolerance and forbearance was the saving of many a (later) career, distinguished or otherwise.

We had fine Police Instructors. Most notable in my mind were Tom Beddis and Jimmy Page. I was, in those days, still a bit smart for my own good at times if I took it into my head to try. Not admirable qualities in a young Police Constable. Tom was my instructor in my last term as a Cadet. I was, again, starting to drift academically near the end of the nineteen months course, and with Finals approaching, I had to start thinking about why I was there. As observed above, I was a great believer in the social side of the course, continuing a fine old time with the guys in my cadet class and the guys I grew up with in Naenae partying, chasing girls etc. I had to start making some choices. Tom had been my coach in the Soccer 2nd XI, my only year at playing soccer, due to a dislocated thumb at the rugby trials. He knew me more than I realised. One day in the last term he called me into his office and ripped into me. He did not appreciate my attempts at humour, my smart attitude, my academic results, pretty much everything about me. I was somewhat taken aback by this. He told me that the rating I was to receive from him would put me back two years in my career. I left that office a sober, quiet young man.

This "chat" stunned me. I respected and liked Tom a lot. He was a very good instructor and a very good man. I felt I had personally let him down. I apologised to him and pulled my head in. That single chat did more to make me grow up than any other experience.

From that point on I was convinced I had failed the course. I worked hard for my finals and passed well. Tom was true to his word though. The course rating could have been a lot better, but was, in hindsight, on the button. The rating caught the attention of Bill Overton, the Superintendent in charge of Lower Hutt, my first posting. I had to explain the rating to him, not an overly pleasant experience! It did not stop my career but probably acted as an incentive to work harder. I thank Tom for that "chat". I have never forgotten it and I like to think it actually made me wake up and get real about the career I was entering. Regretfully Tom died of leukemia a few years after I graduated, leaving a young family.

Jimmy Page was another "legend" in the Police. This short, English ex-soldier, 1937 Lightweight Boxing Champion of Northern China, Ex-Commando Instructor, Hard Man. Jimmy was our drill and PT instructor. He had the No.1 Haircut before people knew what it was. Jimmy had more power and tricks packed into his 5' 5" body than any class of his, sometimes giant, pupils. He was an extremely fair and precise man. Everybody was "Cadet....." Baton training with Jimmy was not an experience one wanted to volunteer for or, if unlucky to be volunteered, ever forget. Jimmy's idea of training was - if you are in the position of inflicting pain you need to experience it as well.

I think Jimmy used to despair at our attempts at drill. We actually became very good over the eighteen months he taught us but the British Grenadiers we were not. In later life Jimmy was a neighbour of mine in Wainuiomata. He never failed to address me as Mr Rattenbury. This used to embarrass me and I wondered if he actually knew my Christian name. I worked up the courage to ask him one day. When he replied "Robert" I was too shy to ask him why he continued to call me by my surname.

24th August 1971, Graduation Day. Seventy one members of my Cadet Wing paraded through the streets of Wellington and graduated at the Wellington Town Hall with the ceremonial replacement of the blue berets with white helmets. We all had our families and then girl-friends present. This was followed with a ball and then postings.

Nineteen months is a long time in a teenager's life. I would not have missed the opportunity I was lucky enough to receive for anything. I met many fine men I still today count as my friends. If I had not managed to enter the Cadets my life could have been worse. It moved me out of my social background, lifting my confidence in myself and my expectations from life. It, overnight, enlarged my social circle to such an extent I can just about guarantee a bed in any town in New Zealand and many countries in the world.

When talking about the Cadet system there is some truth in the concept of developing future leaders. Out of the seventy one graduates from my Cadet Wing thirty two took promotion with seven achieving Commissioned Rank of Inspector or above.

Some chose to remain as Constables or Detectives throughout their careers, becoming strong mentors to younger staff and held in huge respect by all.

Many very able men resigned after a few years to take up challenging positions in business and the professions. They decided that the Police was not enough for them.

Chapter 10

My First Posting
"The old home town looks the same as I step down from the train......"

On 14th September 1971 I began duty as a Probationary Constable at Lower Hutt. My first Sergeant did not like ex-Cadets and made this plain every opportunity he had. I got to walk a lot of beat in Lower Hutt! This is a dormitory town for Wellington and is dead after about 5.00 p.m.

Beat work did not develop me as my contact with the public consisted mainly of chatting up shop-keepers for cups of tea or coffee and shaking door-handles after dark, finding insecure premises. Night shifts were interesting on the beat. If a burglary occurred on your beat and you did not find it you received a "108" or report from this Sergeant asking why it was not found. This did not engender a great deal of loyalty towards your Sergeant.

My section consisted of Constables of various service under the supervision of this Sergeant. Despite the leadership it was a happy section with some hard cases on it. Guys I remember from then were Mike Burnside, Lloyd Te Kani, Stan Hooper, John Dursley, Daphne Pomare, Alan Beardsley and Phillip Keane.

In the early 1970's the Police were still using the five week roster for section staff. This roster had been in place for many years and consisted of seven nights of night shift in a row, three days off then on to what we referred to as late/earlies for three weeks with a week of swing shift thrown in somewhere in the middle. About every five to seven days we would get two days off. In those days we would start duty at 1.00 p.m., our shift finishing at 9.00 p.m. when the night shift would start. We would then be back at 5.00 a.m. to start duty again working until 1.00 p.m. Eight hours between shifts – this gave you time to get home, get to bed, try to sleep, get up again at about 4.00 a.m. and get back to work. A very hard shift to work, complicated even more by perhaps having to work past 9.00 p.m. if you had made an arrest late in the shift. You still had to be on parade again at 5.00 a.m. no matter what time you eventually got to bed. A swing or twilight shift was another type of night shift where we would start work at 7.00 p.m. and supposedly knock off at 3.00 a.m., looking after the pubs and general disorder later in the week on Thursday, Friday and Saturday nights. Invariably we would work on, sometimes to 5.00 a.m. with the night shift.

Concern was being expressed nationally and internationally about the effect these hours had on Police staff long term. I remember just being always tired on the late-early weeks and the night shift weeks. I still managed to work a secondary job as well, so young and fit then. In those days old cops did not tend to last long after retirement, dying within a year of two of retiring at sixty. This was partly put down to the thirty or forty years of constant shift work and broken sleep they put up with. I worked this roster off and on for about fifteen years in various roles. Others worked much longer as well as callouts. The Police were not paid overtime then but could bank hours up to take in lieu when times were quieter.

After some months of walking the beat in Lower Hutt under the anti-ex-cadet Sergeant I had changed sections in early 1972 and began more patrol work with a partner. The Hutt had, in those days, some hardened criminals active in the area. Being from the town was both an aid and a hindrance. My knowledge of criminals was fairly extensive, but I had grown up with them or had lived in the same neighbourhood. This caused problems and resulted in various incidents and arrests.

One I recall was chasing a very well-known burglar over the rooftops of the industrial area of Naenae one evening, catching him on the roof of the RSA just on closing time. We were expressing, with our fists, how much we cared for each other's company when the old soldiers heard the rumpus on the roof. They came out to watch and cheer as "Spider's Boy" and "Ron's Boy the Cop" proceeded to beat the living daylights out of each other. I won when I managed to throw my opponent off the roof. Not very high, and into the arms of my patrol partner waiting below. Neither of us was seriously hurt. Both our fathers were returned men who belonged to the club. Thank God neither was imbibing that late at night. The dents in the roof and spouting were still there when my Dad's funeral service was held at the club twenty six years later. The old boys were still talking about it!

During the course of the next two years stationed at Lower Hutt I attended all forms of incidents as expected of a young Constable. The Hutt station was a very happy place to work with an excellent social life. I found that, whilst I still socialised with school friends and other childhood friends I became more and more involved with the social life of the Police. I moved into Police barracks a few months after graduation, which helped my family. Having a family member on constant shift work and very young children to raise was a bit hard on Mum and Dad. It suited me, more freedom.

When I say Police Barracks, it was really only a flat on the top floor of the Police Station conveniently next door to the Police Bar. It cost me $1.60 per week for my room and I shared the flat with three other Constables, Marty Wright, Ian Weston and Alec Boyd.

Alec was an interesting character. He was the Day Watchhouse Keeper, responsible for stores, running the cells and various other duties that are done on day shift. Alec had been the cop at West Arm in Fiordland when the Manapouri Dam was being built. It was a very tough gig. He used to say he either had to fight or drink a lot of guys into submission. Alec had a very short fuse and used to blow at the drop of a hat. He used to slam phone receivers down on callers in the watch-house so hard he was known to break the receivers in half. He would never send us to domestic disputes if he could help it due to two young cops being shot in Lower Hutt in 1963 while attending a domestic dispute. If he could not solve the issue over the phone he normally just hung up, slamming the phone down, accompanied by a whole list of expletives.

Alec was also a joy to live with, not. Over a period of a couple of weeks the rest of us noticed that our crockery, utensils and pots were disappearing fast from the kitchen. The kitchen was on the top floor overlooking Knights Road and above gardens at the front of the station. Alec used to throw a proper tantrum if we did not wash up after making our meals. One day the Ministry of Works gardeners came into the station with a whole box of crockery, pots, pans and utensils that they had recovered from the garden below our kitchen window. What Alec had done over a period of a couple of weeks was simply open the window at the end of the bench and push all the dirty dishes, pots and utensils left by yours truly and his mates out the second storey window so that they landed in the garden below. He was a cranky old bugger.

Alec got very sick and it was confirmed that he was suffering from non-treatable Leukaemia. I remember him telling me in the bar one night. He said his GP had told him to stop drinking. He then finished his double gin and brought another one. Alec was only about thirty nine when he died but he looked twice that. On the night he died he actually had dinner with Jenny and me at a local restaurant before heading back to barracks where he died in Ian Weston's arms about an hour later in the passage outside his room.

Alec's was the first of quite a few Police funerals I attended. He came from a large family of Police and was, overall a great guy but very unwell. I stayed in the barracks flat for a few more months after Alec's death, moving into our own flat about the time Jenny and I got engaged.

Phil

The day I started as a nineteen year old probationary Constable at Lower Hutt Police station in September 1971 I was met by another probationary, Philip Keane. Phil had just graduated from the recruit course a week before my cadet graduation. In those days most Police trained as recruits, a twelve week course. Phil was the same age as me and actually had been to school with me at St Bernards Primary before going on to St Pat's College in Silverstream. His Dad had been the local Magistrate (District Court Judge nowadays) but had recently passed away.

Phil was, and is, one the greatest characters I have ever met. He did not stay in the Police very long, going on to university and then a very successful career in the private sector in Canada and Australia. He is a really great friend and was one of my groomsmen at Jenny and my wedding in 1973.

Phil is the first to agree that he was not really cut out for Police work. He is a laugh a minute and got me into more trouble than I care to remember. They split us up after a few months putting me on another section. He loves driving very fast on motor cycles and in high performance cars. This sometimes crept into his police work. He is still, forty five years later, famous in Lower Hutt for writing off three Police cars in one accident. One night shift the section was chasing a suspected stolen car along the Petone Esplanade. Phil was not involved, being alone on a mobile beat patrol in Wainuiomata. However, when he heard the radio chatter he decided that he just had to get involved. He sped over the hill with his one red light flashing. We had no sirens in those days, these being removed in the sixties due to improper use by some Police. He did not hear that the car had been caught on top of the Petone overbridge and everything was fine.

He was estimated to be doing about a hundred and fifty km/hour at the roundabout at the bottom of the bridge from the Esplanade when he saw the red lights on top of the bridge. He tried to stop in time, spinning the car into reverse as well, hitting both Police cars on the bridge and missing the chase car completely, cops and the recently nabbed crims jumping out of the way.

All three Police cars were wrecked but thankfully no one was hurt. Phil did not lose his job over this but a few weeks later he had another crash, speeding to Wainuiomata this time and coming to grief in a shop in the corner of Whites Line and

Wainui Road. He got in trouble for that. The final straw in Phil's career was when he wrote the word "wanker" on a notice issued by the Staff Senior Sergeant about leave being cancelled for the upcoming 1973 Springbok Tour (which thankfully never happened). After undertaking handwriting analysis the bosses had a meeting with Phil and discussed with him the possibilities of seeking further employment outside the Police. Phil was still on probation so really had no security anyway. He then resigned.

We still see each other on occasions when he is in New Zealand as he is a really great mate and good friend. He is still as mad as a cut snake at sixty six years of age.

Bit of fun

I was walking the beat on night shift in Lower Hutt one fine Sunday night in late 1971, wondering to myself where I would get my next cup of coffee from. I was about the only person around in the wee hours and had shaken hands with all the door handles in High Street. I was also thinking about nipping off to a quiet wee place us beat cops used to use for a wee snooze as I had a secondary job to go to in the morning and could do with some sleep. Secondary employment was a big thing for cops in those days, working in another job to try to make more money for a house purchase or whatever. It was illegal under the Police Regulations but everybody did it. Myself and another guy from my cadet course, Marty Wright, drove a general freight truck for a local contractor between us as we were on different shifts. Hard work but kept us very fit so sleep was always a priority.

I heard this rhythmical squeaking behind me and looked over my shoulder to find a monkey riding a very small bicycle along the footpath about twenty five metres behind me. I looked again, wondering if I was seeing things. I turned around and the little fellow leapt off his bike, threw it over his shoulder and scampered down an alley way. I thought maybe I have had too much coffee. I could not find him when I went to look in the alley so I just pretended it did not happen and went on my way.

About five minutes later it happened again. This time I chased the little bugger down an alley and into Queens Drive where I saw him climb into a black Holden – the night shift Crime car.

The little monkey was Detective Tata Parata, one of the best practical jokers I ever met. He was completely dressed in a monkey suit and had a small circus bike.

He pulled the stunt again the following week on another beat cop after getting me to keep quiet about it. This beat cop returned to the station and got some green filing tape. When asked by his Sergeant why he was back in the station when he should have been on his beat he said he was going to catch the little monkey and bring it back to the station!

Tata was well known for his gags around the station. Once he somehow acquired an Internal Affairs letterhead and wrote a letter to the Officer in Charge, Police Station, Knights Road, Lower Hutt directing him to arrange for a survey on the amount of toilet paper being used over a period (I think a certain week was mentioned) as part of a nationwide survey on toilet paper usage in government departments. He somehow got Superintendent Bernie Kelly and a Senior Sergeant, Leo Maher, to minute the memo, Leo sending it to a particularly loyal, conscientious and gullible Sergeant to compete the enquiry. Most of us were in on the gag and we would spend far too much time watching this Sergeant walk around the station interviewing people about the average amount of paper used.

In those days Policewomen were not as numerous as now and they had their own office and facilities. No male was allowed into this sanctum.

The Sergeant was seen trying to interview a young female Constable on the use of the toilet paper in the WD's WC. WD is short for Women's Division for those of you too young to remember or know. He was becoming quite insistent and the young Constable was becoming quite concerned, "why was this strange man wanting to know about my toilet habits?"

At about this time Leo took the Sergeant into the office with Tata to let him in on the joke. He was ok with it but we all felt a bit sorry for him as he was a good little guy.

Tata and Leo both passed recently, both great guys and great practical jokers. I was privileged to have known them both.

Women in the Police

When I began as a cadet at the Police Training School in Trentham in January 1970 one of the first lectures we received from our Sergeant Instructor was about the Policewomen undertaking training. We were told in no uncertain terms to keep away from them as they were very busy studying and did not need distractions from spotty faced little schoolboy erks like us.

They were all "older women" to us anyway so most of us did not give it another thought at the time. Some Police dogs were even older than us in those days.

The WDs, as they were known in those days, had their own little barracks block right by the Instructor's block. They lived in one end of the World War 1 hut and advanced courses, usually dog handlers, lived in the other end with a reinforced and locked concrete door in between, or so we were told.

For most of us not a second immoral thought crossed our chaste little minds. However as time went by one or two of the older and more mature-looking cadets, the ones who could shave daily, began to think perhaps they may be able to offer one or more of these ladies a nice night out. The rest of us laughed, all secretly jealous of the "bewhiskered ones" and also still a bit over-awed by the sight of these sophisticated and highly unattainable goddesses on our very distant horizons. I am sure one or two great friendships were begun but discretion and loyalty forbids any further comment.

Time went by in a flash and in August 1971 I arrived at my first posting with a funny hat on my head to be met by Constable Daphne Te Rauoriwa Pomare, my new work buddy. Daphne was an older woman, very worldly-wise and was like an aunty to all of us still very young ex-cadets and nineteen year old ex-recruits. She was a particular mentor and confidant to other, very young and maybe not-so-young Policewomen at the Hutt.

She stuck up for us against the Sergeant who had a particular dislike for life-forms known as ex-cadets, leaving him a bumbling mess at times. She made us go to very proper parties at her place where only the best behaviour was countenanced. She encouraged our friendships with young women that she approved of and counselled us about the others not approved of.

She could have all her male colleagues eating out of her hand at the drop of a hat. She was a woman of steely reputation but with the greatest sense of humour and sense of what was right. She approved very highly of my choice of girlfriend, my now darling wife of forty five years, and acted as an aunty and mentor to Jenny as well.

Daphne and I descend from the same part of New Zealand and it was she who encouraged me to have the courage explore these roots further. Daphne left section after a short while and began working in the Youth Aid Section. In the late 1970s Daphne left the Police and joined Fergie Pickens and other very capable Police to form the Airport Security Service in Wellington.

I lost touch with Daphne for many years, as happens with old cops, until about three years ago we re-established contact via social media. By this time Daph was retired and living in Levin. We talked often on FaceBook or Messenger or whatever. I knew she was in Perth seeing whanau and was looking forward to catching up again when she got home, perhaps travelling down to Levin with Jen and visiting her. On 23 October 2016 Daphne was killed in a motor accident at Paekakariki on the way home to Levin from the airport.

Daphne and other strong women such as my CIB In-Service Training Instructor, Jean Dougall, taught me to value, respect and admire Police women in a time when this was maybe not the case as it should have been.

Times have changed now, for the better thankfully, and women will soon, I hope, comprise 50% of the Police. They have stormed the last bastions of maleness, AOS and Dog Section, welcomed with open arms (in an appropriate way of course) by their male colleagues.

Women had it tough in the Police in the 1970's and 1980's but they were, by and large, brighter, more motivated, certainly nicer to look at, than most of their male colleagues. They also smelled nicer.

I had left the Police before I had a female manager. In a later life I worked for an organization where males were in the minority, certainly old, grumpy straight ones like me. My managers were all female and what a pleasant change that was. Hard to work for but quick to understand and forgive. They were, without exception, very bright and highly motivated individuals. I saw in these women exactly the same qualities I saw in Daphne and her peers. The difference was that these women were encouraged to shine and did not have to fight for everything us males assumed.

E noho ra – arohanui e hoa Daphne – we miss you every day my dear friend

Chapter 11

Jenny, Her Family and a Wedding

In mid-1971 a mate of mine from the Police cadets, John Spalding, was injured playing rugby and was admitted to Hutt Hospital. Whilst there tests showed that John had leukemia which was unable to be treated. This was devastating for a 19 year old to deal with. All of us used to visit John regularly. He was a popular guy, great rugby player, ace 500 player and doing very well academically. John decided to remain in the cadets and graduate with us in the August of 1971. He was then posted to Auckland Central where he remained on light duties. Sadly John passed away a short time after graduation. He was a great loss to his family and friends.

The upside to this very sad time was meeting Jennifer Margaret Skeet, a student nurse in John's ward. Jenny was actually going out with a good mate of mine, Peter Mayo and I was also otherwise involved. However I must admit to having my head turned from the time we met. She was the sunniest and most opinionated young woman I had met. She also radiated a basic goodness which everyone recognized. She annoyed me a bit with her directness but I could not stop thinking about her, but in a distant unattainable way.

I managed to dance with Jenny a bit at my graduation ball and fell in love with her. My date was not a keen dancer and a bit needy to say the least. Whatever relationship we had finished that night.

Months and more girlfriends go by. Another cadet mate of mine, Malcolm Bennett, was getting married and invited me to his wedding. I also needed to bring a partner. I was between "friends" at the time so wondered what to do. I knew Peter was seeing someone else. I thought I would see if Jenny would like a good wedding, most girls did in those days. I thought to myself that I had better be careful here, Peter is a mate. I rang Peter and asked him if he minded if I asked Jen to accompany me to Malcolm's wedding. He gave me his blessing which ensured we remained mates.

I took a deep breath and rang the Virgins' Castle (Nurses residence) at Hutt hospital and asked to speak to Jenny Skeet. With a very dry mouth I asked Jenny if she would like to go to a wedding with me. Jenny, of course, jumped at the chance. I seized the day (Carpe diem for those of a more military bent) and also asked her if she would like to go to the pictures with me later that week. She agreed. Jenny was the last girlfriend I ever had.

We kicked around for a while getting to know each other, eventually setting up flat together near the Hutt Hospital. Jenny had to keep her room at the castle as in 1971 it was frowned upon by the Police and the hospital for their young employees to "live in sin". Also Jenny's parents may not have understood. My parents, being the tolerant pair they were, gave us their blessing.

Jenny was a practicing Anglican, ex Sunday school teacher and chorister in her Church, St Mathews, in Masterton. She explained my Catholicism and Maori background to her parents who could not have cared less. This was still a sticky issue with some families in those days, which sounds so silly now.

Obviously my parents had no issue with the difference in denomination. Mum and Dad knew Jenny very well before I started going out with her as she and Peter used to visit often when I was living at home and also after I left home. Mum loved Jen almost from day one.

I remember turning up at Mum's with Jenny one day after we had been going out a short while. Mum looked over my shoulder and asked where Peter was. I told Mum that Jenny and I were seeing each other. Mum was a bit taken aback but approved.

Jenny's relationship with my father was a bit different. Jenny does not usually hold back with her opinions and disagreed with Dad a lot about a great many things. Dad, being your basic home-grown misogynist, was not used to this and used to get a bit grumpy. Jenny also would not put up with the old man's behaviour when he had been drinking. This was like a red rag to a bull with Dad and usually resulted in him storming out of the room, much to everyone's amusement. I think they learned to respect each other eventually.

Jenny graduated from her Nursing course and we continued living in our little flat on the corner of Kings Crescent and High Street, Lower Hutt with Jenny maintaining her room at the castle. I eventually worked up the courage to ask Jenny for her hand in marriage.

We were so young, Jenny was nineteen and I was twenty. Jenny agreed to marry me of course, she knew she was on a winner. We then went to Masterton and took her Dad Joe to the Soldiers Club, shouted him a jug and I asked for Jenny's hand in marriage. Joe agreed. Jenny's mum Pam was also very happy about this turn of events so we were engaged in October 1972.

Pam was worried about our youth which was very understandable. Both of us were at school within the last two to three years.

Jenny's family home is in Landsdowne, Masterton. Her dad Joe was an electrician by trade and fought in World War 2 as a tankie in the New Zealand 2nd Division, mainly in Italy. He had a bad war, not that there is ever a good war. I liked Joe a lot and respected him greatly for his quietness, shyness, skills with his hands and his advice on looking after my car properly. He was a wonderful father to his children Jenny, Elizabeth, Gillian and Andrew. He was a great gardener and home handyman and, when I knew him, worked for the New Zealand Post and Telegraph branch in Masterton as an electrician.

Joe's health suffered due to his war experiences. He never liked to talk about his time in Italy. He would just say "war solves nothing" and then clam up.

Over the years I spent many happy hours playing snooker with Joe at the Masterton Soldiers Club where he was a popular and very respected member. Joe was not a big drinker, usually having a jug over about an hour or so then home. He liked a wee whisky at Christmas as well but was otherwise a very quiet-living family man.

One ANZAC Day years ago we travelled from Whanganui to Masterton with the kids to see Pam and Joe. I left the family at home and went to the Soldiers Club to catch up with Joe who was there with his old Army mates. As I walked into the lounge at the club I saw Joe sitting with his old mates, some of whom I had met over the years, all really good solid old guys. Joe was crying. I asked one of his mates, Mr O'Donnell, what was wrong. He told me that they were talking about a group of their schoolboy mates who were burned to death in their tank in front of Joe in Italy after the Germans had hit the tank with shellfire. Joe was trying to get them out but could not help. They were alive and knew what was happening to them. All these men had grown up and gone to school together. They were all close friends and good mates.

Nearly fifty years later Joe was still suffering from the experience. Post-Traumatic Stress Disorder, if not treated, never goes away. These ex-soldiers came home deeply scarred by their war time experiences and the only support and therapy they had was each other and booze. Joe's mates at the table were trying to reassure him that there was nothing that he could have done to save their friends and that it was not his fault. Mr O'Donnell told me that it was a regular thing and that Joe had gone through hell overseas. Joe never told his children about this. I told Jenny and Andrew after Joe died as he did not want them to know.

These old warriors did not want their children or wives to be worried about their awful experiences. They bottled things up with the expected outcome for many, nervous disorders, drinking problems, family violence and early death.

Joe died in 1998 at the age of seventy six, a brave old soldier at rest at last. I came to love him and, as stated, deeply respected his bravery and his wish to not let his family know too much about his war.

Jenny's Mum Pamela Letts is an English woman, a "ten pound Pom" who came to New Zealand in 1950 to work as a nurse. She met Joe and decided to stay thankfully. Pam grew up in Weybridge, Surrey with her widowed mother and siblings. I have met all her siblings and they were a tough-minded focused bunch but I liked them immensely. Pam trained as a Registered Nurse at the Royal Berkshire Hospital in Reading, riding her bicycle to work during air raids so that she could help with the injured. She was a very brave young woman who worried her family a lot. As an aside she also got fresh fruit if she went to work, very important in the days of rationing.

Later after the war, Pam worked for Dr Archie McIndoe, a New Zealand Plastic Surgeon, at his plastic surgery hospital at East Grinstead, Sussex, nursing mainly RAF personnel suffering from terrible burns and requiring plastic surgery. Dr McIndoe preferred employing young attractive and chatty nurses to try to lift the spirits of the young men he was treating. These men were horribly disfigured by their injuries with the resultant loss of self-esteem so part of the therapy was to be able to chat with young women who did not judge them but who cared for them in a professional way. He also ensured that there were kegs of beer in every ward for the young guys to enjoy in a responsible manner as going to the local pubs was sometimes an issue for these brave young men.

When Pam married Joe she returned to nursing after having the children and worked as a midwife at Masterton Hospital for many years until she retired. She was remembered as a strong no-nonsense nurse who loved the babies and offered very sound advice and support to the young mothers and student nurses working with her.

Pamela is very intelligent and was educated privately on a scholarship at William Perkins School in Chertsey, a big thing for a middle class girl from Weybridge. She raised all her children to be intelligent, outspoken and caring individuals.

Jenny and her siblings all have strong opinions about most things, a trait they inherit from Pam I am sure. They have all done well in life and raised great children as well. At the time of writing this Pam is still alive, 93 and living in a rest home. She still does her word puzzles every day and can still engage in a decent "discussion" breaking into French at times for some reason. Jenny and I try to keep up with our school French but she is still way ahead of us.

Jenny and I got married on 26 May 1973 at St Mathews Anglican Church in Masterton. My stag party was held in my Uncle Jack McHugh's garage up the road from home on 22 May, my 21st birthday. The only females at my 21st were my dear Mum and Aunty Dot McHugh who were doing the catering. They kept well away from Uncle Jack's garage where the boys were celebrating. I had about a hundred mates there from both the Police and from Naenae. This was interesting as whilst my Naenae mates liked me they did not necessarily have much time for cops. Everybody behaved themselves, well mostly. An old mate, Stefan Polaschek, a tough Polish kid, objected to some of my cop mates dumping me on the ground for the customary "nuggetting" and things got a bit busy for a while. No worries, a beer or two and they were all old friends again. A few lost buttons and fat lips.

My wedding party consisted of my cousin and very close mate at the time, best man John McHugh, Frazer Tweedie and Philip Keane, two close mates from the Police. Another old Naenae mate, Lance Hartley, was with the group as well. John, Phil, Lance and I were all staying in the same room at a motel prior to the wedding. Frazer and his wife Becky had a room not far from us. On the morning of the wedding someone started a food fight in the boys' motel room which resulted in all of us being thrown out of the motel, suits and all. Just bloody marvellous. We had to hide in Frazer's room all morning until we could walk the short distance to the Church. Naenae boys! – We could not help ourselves despite all having great jobs or at university and with great potential. We still descended into yobbery at the first opportunity. You can take the boy out of Naenae but you cannot take Naenae out of the boy.

The wedding went off well and we had the wedding breakfast at the Masterton Town Hall with the Vicar, Arch-Deacon Vincent Venimore at one end of the main table and my Aunty Pat, or Sister Mary Dominica as she was known as in her religious order, at the other end. They had a great time together, neither hung up on the religious thing.

When Jenny and I visited Arch-Deacon Venimore to talk about the wedding and announcing of the banns he asked me if I was a Christian. I replied that I was, that I attended church regularly still in Naenae. He asked "St David's" and I replied "no, St Bernadette's". He smiled. I liked the guy. I never did get around to contacting the Pope for a dispensation to marry outside my faith. Arch-Deacon Venimore served as a chaplain in the Pacific during the War ministering to all denominations. He retired to Whanganui and on the 25th anniversary of our wedding, in 1998, he wrote to us.

We had invited him personally to the celebration but he was not that well at the time. He had a lot of time for Jenny and her family. He also said at the time "I knew it would last". Arch-Deacon Venimore has since passed as all old soldiers do.

After the wedding breakfast the Rattenbury side of the hall adjourned back to Naenae for a wee Irish hoolie to see the bride and groom off on their honeymoon. We spent the night in the new James Cook Hotel and took the ferry the next day for a road trip around the South Island. Road trips have been a huge feature of our life together, taking the kids all around New Zealand on holidays and then driving around Australia, the USA and the UK over the years, letting the road take us wherever.

After the honeymoon we settled into married life in our little flat, gathering together furniture and bits and bobs. I bought a lounge suite for $6, a beautiful old humpty dumpty suite. I sold it to a mate for $10 when we ordered and received our brand new $400 leather suite made especially for us. The first items we brought were the bedroom suite (of course) a cheap table and chairs and a fridge to keep the food (beer) in.

We both carried on working, partying and being involved in family activities until we transferred to Masterton in October 1973.

On 16th September 1975 our eldest child and the first grandchild of both families, the beautiful wee Jodie Leanne, arrived, taking her time and putting her mother through all sort of bother during labour. Jodie was followed on 2nd June 1981 by our lovely and very brave son Luke Euan, a lively wee man who gave his mum no trouble at all during labour. He has not stopped still since.

Jenny has been my strongest support and friend all my adult life. Our love for each other is at least as strong today as it was when we were young people trying to find our way. Jenny has saved my life by nagging me to go to the doctor, resulting in me being diagnosed with testicular cancer. If I had been single or with a woman who did not have Jenny's training I would probably have left matters too late.

Jenny supported my Police career, placing her own career on hold and leaving really good jobs to follow my moves in the Police. She is a wonderful mother to our kids and is now demanding grandchildren from them as payback.

I consider myself to be the luckiest man in the world to have a wife like my sunny, gorgeous, good, maddening, hard-working, focused petal Jenny. I love her so much.

Chapter 12

The country life for me

In October 1973, five months after we married, following a need to save some money, Jenny and I transferred to Masterton. The job had a house with a low rental of $16 per week. As we were paying $32 per week for our flat in Lower Hutt this was too good to be true. Jenny is from Masterton and I had a few mates stationed there. It was my first experience of "country life" and we loved it. There was plenty of secondary employment to make extra money towards our own home too.

Jenny obtained a nursing job at Masterton Hospital and we settled into a life revolving around shifts, me working the dreaded five week roster then in place nationally, long hours of work and serious socialising. I had obtained my permanent appointment just prior to the transfer so employment was secure. In those days obtaining permanent appointment was not a formality. Failing to perform satisfactorily in the two years following graduation or failing the permanent appointment exam resulted in deferment for three months. Further failure resulted in dismissal. I sat my exam on my honeymoon, having to cut it short to return to the North Island to sit the exam in Wellington. The Department, in its wisdom, would not let me sit the exam in Christchurch with my ex-Cadet colleagues. No reason was given, but it was a good chance to stuff up a young man's honeymoon so let us do it anyway. Some would call this bad planning on my behalf. I prefer to think that I was naive enough to believe that the part of the Police responsible for Permanent

Appointment exams was ruled by common sense.

My time in Masterton was a learning experience. I had the pleasure of working under the supervision of two excellent Sergeants, Henricus Egbertus Bos and Bob Atkinson. Both were outstanding leaders in their own different ways. Ric was outgoing, loud, mercurial, unconventional, Dutch, and LOYAL. He looked after us young cops like a father. He was quick to lecture us about our shortcomings, but stuck up for us when the shit started to fly. Bob, being an ex-Cadet, knew every trick in the book in handling young cops. He lead from the front and expected his staff to be loyal, hard-working and accountable.

Masterton in the early seventies was a busy town with fencing and shearing gangs visiting town regularly to drink and play up. These were tough guys who worked in physically demanding jobs. They had no love for cops and were not slow in showing it when drunk. I learned how to use my Irish charm and cute good looks to my advantage but at times we took our knocks and limped off into the darkness to fight another day. I discovered the power of the summons. When one is outnumbered ten to one remember the offences committed and those responsible. Visit them the next day when they are crook with the booze and serve them with a summons for fighting, disorderly behaviour etc. It saved a lot of sweat and blood (usually mine).

In the early 1970s Masterton had a population of around 19,000. The Police in the town numbered about twenty five, all up, including CIB, civilians and day shift workers. Sectional staff on the five week roster numbered about fifteen in total. These fifteen staff were split into five sections of three. Of these at any one time five could be on annual leave so most sections only had two Constables, one in the station looking after the prisoners and answering the emergency 111 line and one outside responding to all calls involving crime. On some occasions, especially night shifts, the Constable could be accompanied by the Masterton Civil Defence Policeman, Sonny Lusty or the Maori Warden Whare Mitchell. In the pre- merger days the Ministry of Transport usually had one Traffic Officer on after 5.00 p.m. but he was gone by 10.00 p.m. On the odd occasions I would team up with the on duty Traffic Officer in his car, a V8 Holden with a siren, a lot more use than our HQ 6 cylinder Holdens with no sirens.

Staffing was always an issue in those days but we made do with what we had and just boxed on. The three Uniform Branch Sergeants worked days and late shift with one working through to about 2.00 a.m. on Friday and Saturday nights.

If you were the Constable on patrol on your own you had to deal with everything. Being a rural area this also meant dealing with dogs attacking stock, poaching, farm accidents and serious motor crashes in the rural areas surrounding Masterton, a very large area indeed.

Assaults on Police were rife at that time. Our local Police Association (Union) Committee was pushing for more Constables to be stationed in Masterton due to the heavy work load we carried and the danger the staff faced. On one occasion they undertook a three month survey of assaults on Police. In the three months the fifteen Constables on the section strength were assaulted bad enough to warrant arresting the offender a total of twenty five occasions, almost two assaults per person. This did not take into account the members who were on leave and included in that fifteen. I went through quite a few shirts and ties when in Masterton.

Nowadays with not much more of a population I understand that Masterton can field up to five Constables on any one shift with a Sergeant on each of the five sections to look after them, which is great.

Wayne Harris was a young Constable working with me on section at Masterton. He had graduated from the cadets a year after me. Wayne was married and was reconsidering his future in the Police.

He had decided to resign and was working his notice out. We were walking the beat in Queen Street when a well-known little criminal, Jimmy Scott, began playing up, just annoying antics that required a quiet word. My off-sider was a bit of a runner and when Scott refused to talk to us and ran off we took off after him. Wayne, being fleeter than me, caught Scott in a carpark behind some shops.

By the time I caught up Scott had flattened Wayne and was putting the boot in. I arrested Scott, during the course of which a struggle ensued (your Honour). Scott managed to acquire some head injury that required hospitalisation. No, I did not baton him. Unfortunately for me Scott belonged to a well-known family of criminals who were not used to members receiving injuries from the Constabulary.

That evening seven members of the family began visiting Police Officers homes in an attempt to identify and deal to the cop responsible for decking their darling. They turned up at my home and failed to identify me. Jenny and I then moved into my in-laws while an enquiry began into their behaviour. The seven were arrested and charged with unlawful assembly and conspiracy to assault me. They were ably represented by Trevor de Cleene, later an MP, and found guilty. The old darling of a Magistrate fined them as I was a Police Officer and should expect problems like this!

This habit of visiting and besetting homes of Police was a peculiarly Masterton thing to do. It later developed into fire-bombings etc. In such a small town the crims always made it their business to know where Police lived, where their wives worked and where their children went to school.

Subsequently my dealings with this family were fraught with problems. I had to keep dealing with them as they were responsible for a lot of the crime committed in the town. The oldest brother, Sonny, was especially dangerous. We concentrated on them for a while and they went quiet.

About twelve years later Sonny was arrested in Wanganui for shop-breaking. I was a sectional Sergeant in Wanganui at the time and I made myself known to Sonny. We had a grand old chat about the case. Sonny was a "good" criminal who did not have much time for his younger brother. I think deep down he thought the young bugger needed a tune up. We parted on good terms and it settled things between us.

While we were in Masterton we purchased a section in Carterton with, perhaps, a view of building our first home there. I worked several secondary jobs to make extra money including hay-making, fruit-picking, truck-driving, being a blockie's labourer and helping to build tennis courts with a contractor. We sold the section upon leaving Masterton, making a very healthy profit which put us into our first home in Wainuiomata.

I applied in mid-1974 to enter the Criminal Investigation Branch

(CIB) as a Constable on Trial. To be accepted I would have to attend a CIB Induction Course at Trentham. This seemed a natural progression for me after about three years in uniform as a Constable. I enjoyed working on some serious crime enquiries I had been involved in while in Masterton and a few of my mates were joining the CIB so I thought why not give it a go. It would mean us having to transfer back to Wellington but we were young.

First I had to undergo an interview with the Regional Head of the CIB. I was duly summonsed from Masterton to Wellington to be interviewed by Superintendent "Sport" Cook, a charming old duffer who epitomised the old time detective. I was late for the interview as my rail car broke down. This did not help matters. After undergoing a grilling on statutes and explaining my arrest record for the previous twelve months I was tersely told by Mr Cook that I would be contacted in due course and that punctuality is a requirement of a good detective!

Chapter 13

How NOT to plan a successful career in the Police

In January 1975 I began my CIB induction course. On the course was one of my Cadet mates, Ross Pinkham. This was the second such course run by the Police, the first one resulting in seven failures out of twenty four course members. I knew some of these seven guys and they were good cops. I did not rate my chances too highly. The course was extremely challenging with a pass mark of 80% in every test or exam.

After four weeks we were still all together. It was a course where you were expected to work in the evenings, but also to socialise, as every good detective knows, most information comes from informants in hotels. We had to practise drinking. I had no problem with this part of the course.

After the final exams we were marched in individually and interviewed by the Course Co-ordinators Brian Hartley and Rex Miller. It was explained to me that my strength in investigations was my ability to get on with people and to obtain information. I was told that I had the makings of a good practical cop and would, with time, become an excellent investigator. I could have told them that before the bloody four week course. It was not until the final course "function" that we were all told that we had passed.

I returned to Uniform duties in Masterton pending a vacancy in the CIB in Wellington.

In May 1975 we transferred back to Wellington, getting a Police house in Waitangirua, Porirua. We were the only people in our street whose first language was English. Upon starting in the Wellington CIB as a Constable on Trial I was assigned to the Indecency Squad under the supervision of Detective Sergeant Ted Lines. Ted is a great guy and great teacher. He was very quiet and methodical. I shared my days with such luminaries as Brian Toomey, Ray Whitham and Trevor Morley - brilliant detectives. Also in the office were two class mates from St Bernard's College days, Tim Belcher and John Kelly, also trainee detectives. Ross also started in the CIB office the same day as me as well.

The office was under the control of Detective Senior Sergeant Colin "Pancho" Lines, Ted's brother. How this man and Ted could be brothers never failed to amaze me. Pancho or "the Captain" had a unique management style – his way or the highway. He and I did not hit it off from the start for some reason. Sometimes in life this happens and that was how it was with us. This did not bode well for my career both then and in the future.

I worked very hard, obtaining my Detective Constable designation after six months and doing well at In Service Training. This was a course of units that had to be passed with that old 80% mark to retain your position in the office. I really enjoyed the work and, after a few months, found myself on Crime Squad working a twenty four hour roster with a qualified Detective. Over the next eighteen months or so I acquired a great deal of experience in dealing with serious crime. I also worked on Car Squad with Detective Sergeant Pat Moore, a very able young detective who reached very high rank. In those days the motor cycle gangs were prolific and the theft of English motor cycles was rife. My role on the Car Squad was to follow up the thefts of motor cycles. This involved obtaining information from the underworld about the whereabouts of the stolen bikes and parts and then getting search warrants to visit the addresses, hopefully finding stolen property and arresting offenders. The gangs were quite sophisticated in those days and used to re-stamp chassis numbers and engine numbers and then legally register the bikes. We would still take bikes and ask the DSIR to carry out out metallurgy testing on the numbers. This would show whether or not the chassis or engine numbers had been re-stamped. This was interesting work which resulted in the conviction of a few bikies for theft or receiving while I was doing the job. I had my own storeroom at the old Central Police Station in Waring Taylor Street crammed with motor cycles and parts.

To qualify as a Detective in the CIB in New Zealand a trainee starts as a Constable on Trial for six months after successfully passing the CIB induction course. At the end of that period if all is well the trainee is designated a Detective Constable and continues working on different squads for a further two years.

During this time the trainee also undertakes fairly intensive study on criminal investigation techniques, law, evidence and practical duties as a detective. The very high standard of the 80% pass mark is applied throughout the training. Failure to pass the units of study at any stage will result in the trainee leaving the CIB for general duties in uniform. At the end of the two and a half years of study and trial the trainee then has to attend a Detective Qualifying Course at the Police College and pass this at the old 80%. If this happens and all other things being equal, such as manager's reports on the trainee then the designation of Detective is received.

Shortly after starting in the CIB Jenny and I bought our first home in Wainuiomata. Jenny was expecting Jodie, our first child and life was great. Because of the distance to Wellington and the long hours I was doing I began thinking of a transfer to Lower Hutt CIB. It became apparent after a short while that I was, at that time, a bit low in the pecking order to achieve the transfer. If I had pulled my head in and waited I would have moved to the Hutt within the year. However that Irish rush of blood mixed with a dose of Taranaki Maori resulted in me resigning from the CIB and applying for a transfer back to the Uniform Branch. I had been led to believe that this would result in a transfer back to the Hutt. I was wrong. I got sent to the Uniform Branch in Wellington Central. Not only was I out of the CIB but I was back on straight shift work, the dreaded five week roster again, lost my allowances, and to top it off, because I was perceived as being a bit disruptive I was sent to the Police information section at Knigges Avenue. Further to go each day! I had no one to blame but myself. Bugger!

I was at a bit of a loose end career-wise. I had made a bad call and did not have the maturity or wisdom to speak to the right people in an effort to correct things. If I had approached Jean Dougall, my In Service Training Instructor, or Wally Baker, the head of the CIB I would probably have stayed in the CIB. At twenty three years of age I found these people quite intimidating to approach so let matters rest.

While cooling my heels at Knigges Avenue I saw a vacancy for an explosive detector dog handler. This looked like straight hours with, perhaps, a vehicle thrown in. I had a dog and enjoyed working with her. I put the application in, was interviewed by Chief Inspector Ian Mills, the deputy Director of Operations and got the job.

Chapter 14

Life with Dogs

The late 1970's were unusual times with Robert Muldoon as Prime Minister of New Zealand and international terrorism making itself felt in Australia and here via the Ananda Marga Sect. Coincidentally the Police decided to train and deploy three explosive detector dogs operationally. Search dogs were already operational in New Zealand as narcotic detectors in the Police and the Customs Department, proving very successful.

The explosive detector dog teams were to be based in Auckland, Wellington and Christchurch and cover the country and potentially the Pacific region.

In about December 1976 Ian Kennard from Auckland, Paul Kane from Christchurch and me met at the Trentham Police Dog School. Ian and I knew each other from Cadet training, him being a year behind me. Paul was an older and very experienced dog handler with many years in the Section.

We were allocated a German Shepherd dog each, mine being the only bitch of the three. The dogs were re-named, Cord (Auckland), Nitro (Christchurch) and Dyna (Wellington). Dyna had been born at the kennels and was eighteen months old when allocated to me. She was a very placid little dog but had never been properly socialized until then so we spent many hours walking the streets, getting used to cars, loud noises and lots of children wanting to pat her. As she was so docile and cute she was used for "hands on" sessions with school-children. As we all know, some Police dogs are probably not of a mind to allow this to happen.

The three dogs were not trained on man-work (to bite and maul). As search dogs their only aim in life was to work in an undistracted way with their handlers.

We spent several months, including two courses at Trentham, training with Allan Symes, a Welshman but an ex-English Police dog handler who helped to start the NZ Police dog Section working under Sergeant Frank Riley, also an ex-English handler from Surrey. Allan was most gifted at animal training. Some said he could train a gold fish to stand on its' head. Colin Guppy was also one of the first instructors at the Dog School. Gups was to be my supervisor in the Wellington Dog Section. Great guy.

We spent some time on an explosives course with the NZ Army Ordnance Corps, identifying and handling explosives. The course instructor was an English army captain recently sent on secondment to the New Zealand Army after several tours in Belfast's bomb disposal unit. The Army also took responsibility for supplying and storing our training samples of gelignite, plastic PE4 explosive and Metabyl sheet plastic. We also eventually trained the dogs to detect black powder. All explosive substances have distinctive smells easily detected by dogs, even when very well hidden. The dogs can also indicate where explosives may have been stored and later removed.

In about February 1977 we were trained enough to be cleared as operational for full duties on bomb detection work, assisting in the execution search warrants and Diplomatic Protection work, searching and clearing buildings and areas prior to VIPs arriving.

We were initially part time handlers as the concept was new. I also worked as one of the Property Officers at Wellington Central Police Station. We were each allocated an old surplus Police vehicle to carry the mutts around in, my first was an ex-CIB plain car with a wooden floor in the back where the seats used to be. We eventually graduated to old marked Police dog vans that no-one else wanted. Whilst we were part of the Police Dog Section we tended to work more with the Narcotic Detector Dog handlers, our training systems being a little similar.

During late 1977 we all went back to the Dog School to train the dogs to also detect firearms and ammunition, this making us a much more attractive proposition as aides to general duties and CIB staff.

We also became full time handlers about this time as work was increasing and none of us was spending much time at our normal Police jobs.

Dyna had the first find of explosives when we were executing a search warrant at a safe-cracker's address in Naenae in mid-1977. The cracksman had wrapped up several sticks of gelignite in newspaper and plastic and buried them in his compost heap. Dyna indicated virtually straightway by sitting next to the heap. I should say here that the bomb dogs were not trained to dig out finds for obvious reasons. When they detected an explosive or firearm they sit. Amazing really.

Within a week or two the other two dogs had also had finds. This lent credibility to the new idea with investigative staff so our workloads increased a lot. The cracksman got a lengthy term of imprisonment for this and other charges preferred.

All the dogs went on to find a lot of evidence over the following years. We were very lucky in that every bomb alert we went to was unsuccessful thankfully. Never found a bomb BUT....Next instalment!!

Ananda Marga -

Robert Muldoon as Prime Minster was a divisive figure in New Zealand history. He was hated by many and probably misunderstood by many. Threats against him were ongoing so Dyna and I spent a lot of time at Parliament or at Vogel House and travelling the country with Muldoon's security team, especially during the 1978 General Election lead up.

At about this time a sect called Ananda Marga was active in Australia and New Zealand. In Australia they were responsible for the Hilton Hotel bombing in Sydney in 1978 where three people, including a police officer, were killed. Two members of the Ananda Marga sect had blown themselves up in Auckland in the mid 1970s while transporting a bomb for some purpose.

In New Zealand members of the sect were also caught trying to break into an explosive store at Horokiwi quarry, near Lower Hutt, by Constable Neville Sawyer one night. Neville was kidnapped by the group, eventually being released physically unharmed but very shaken. I cannot remember the outcome of this incident but I think one or two were imprisoned for kidnapping. The aim of the group at the time was to bomb the Indian Embassy in Lower Hutt.

These dudes were serious and motivated terrorists. But things were played down at the time. Their main issue was with India and it's political system. They would target venues or events where Indian government officials may be attending. It was due to this group that the Police stationed an armed Constable at the Indian Ambassador's residence in Lower Hutt for many years.

One fine day I was told to help the Diplomatic Protection Squad clear the grounds and buildings at Vogel House in Lower Hutt, the then Prime Minister's official residence, as some big cheese from India was coming for some kai with Muldoon. No worries. Dyna trotted off to do her thing, scanning the beautiful gardens and grounds on the property until she got to a macrocarpa hedge situated about five metres from the side of Vogel House where the function was to take place. She then poked her head into the four metre high hedge, withdrew it and sat!!!

Shit!

Dyna was very reliable, as most search dogs are. She had never let the team down before, in fact the opposite. The DPS cop and I immediately took several long strides in the opposite direction, radioed the team in the house (probably not a good idea when I think about it) and told them to evacuate the building. Muldoon was not happy but obliged reluctantly.

We then re-grouped and after a while I had Dyna do the search again, starting well away from the spot but with some very important figures watching this time. The Indians were en route and their motorcade had to be diverted. Dyna got to the spot where she had earlier indicated and did the same thing, sat. I offered my opinion that there was an explosive present or there had been recently. At the time we had not approached the hedge for obvious reasons. The Army Bomb team turned up in about an hour and sent a wheelbarrow robot to have a look. Nothing was found other than some disturbed ground inside the hedge.

I was satisfied that there had been explosives present at some stage prior to our search and I was strongly supported by the very senior Police then present and also the Army guys who also operated these dogs. We had a scientist from the DSIR do a subsequent check which did not rule out explosives but was inconclusive. A scenario was posited that a device had been planted with the intention of exploding while the Indian VIP was present at Vogel House, but for some reason it was removed. Police had information at the time that the Ananda Marga was planning something but no details were revealed.

Muldoon grizzled and went back into the house for a stiff gin. By this time it was about 4.30 in the afternoon and the Indians decided to not come for lunch.

Dyna dog was a heroine and seemed quite pleased with herself for causing all this kerfuffle. She got an extra biscuit that night and was allowed to watch TV a little later than normal.

Over the years we worked together Dyna and I spent many hours at Vogel House. The Prime Minister and his wife Thea lived in a flat on the top floor of the home and on the odd occasion Mrs Muldoon would ask for me to bring Dyna up to her flat as she liked to spoil her. Dyna got tidbits and pats while I got to stand awkwardly in the corner of the room while Muldoon usually glared at me or totally ignored me and carried on reading or watching TV. No small talk. Mrs Muldoon was a very nice person who liked a chat but we never stayed long.

God Squad

In the late seventies a commune was set up in North Canterbury near Waipara by a group calling itself the God Squad. I cannot remember and really am not that interested in what the philosophy of these nutters was but I know it was intended to involve an armed stand-off at the commune for some reason.

Many members of the God Squad were serving RNZAF personnel in Canterbury and the Manawatu with one or two groups' in Wellington.

The Police set up a very covert operation in about 1978 to execute search warrants on all the groups addresses nationally at the same time and to deal with what appeared to be serving armed forces personnel involved in a plot to undertake some form of violence and mayhem on a national level.

The Police worked with the Air Force and Army Military Police units who assisted with enquiries and warrants on the Air Force bases, particularly at Ohakea.

Dyna dog and I assisted in executing search warrants in Lower Hutt, in and near Bulls, Dannevirke and Whanganui. The other two dog teams also did the same in their areas. At one address in Woburn, Lower Hutt, we found a house literally packed with black powder, ammunition and weapons. It was incredible what these guys had. Also tactical equipment apparently purloined from the military. The weapons were civilian rifles and shotguns.

Searches at the other addresses also revealed a large number of similar weapons, ammunition and powder. Explanations were not readily forthcoming from the Air Force personnel involved.

My involvement was confined to working as an aide to then Detective Chief Inspector Alan Galbraith who ran the enquiry from Palmerston North. Alan and his wife kindly put me up at their home during the operation as he did not want it advertised that there were outside Police in town.

The Air Force personnel were all dealt with either under military law or the civil law and had their careers terminated by the Defence force. Some were jailed. During the course of the searches we also uncovered a lot of stolen military property.

This was quite a big deal at the time.

Sick Puppy

As a dog handler I had to keep a close eye on what Dyna dog ate. She could be a bit sneaky and the odd smelly dead hedgehog might find itself on the menu if I was not careful. As a search dog Dyna worked inside all sorts of homes from the scungiest druggie bedsit to mansions owned by rich criminals so it was important that we did not have any wee "mistakes" while we were bouncing around in someone else's home having the time of our lives.

One cold wintry Wellington day I was called to an address on the Terrace with Her Highness to undertake a search warrant with the guys and gals from the Wellington CIB under the Arms Act and Summary Proceedings Act. Muttsie had not been well for a couple of days, I think a bit of dead wildlife had been consumed, anyway the poor girl had the trots and was a bit out of sorts.

But she was a working dog so off we went. The address was owned by a very important guy, so he says. It was a beautifully decorated and furnished mansion and he was a complete twit. The team was there to look for weapons this clown was reported to be importing into New Zealand to sell to underworld figures.

Upon arrival at the address we were stopped by the guy from entering as he did not want a smelly dog and equally disreputable-looking handler wandering around his palace. I was actually on annual leave, dressed roughly and bearded. He was soon put right by the team and away we went. He was trying to be present everywhere throughout the house as he thought the team of cops was going to plant evidence. It was quite funny really as it was a huge house and he was a very fat and unfit man, running up and down stairs, yelling and performing like a trained seal.

Dyna dog was not impressed by this chap the way he was shouting at her boss. I sent her up a very well-carpeted stairway, gold shag pile no less. The princess got to the top of the stairs, turned around and looked at me, (I am sure she winked) did that little pirouette she always did before number twos and deposited a very large runny stinking brown mass on the gold shag pile. I was of course telling her she was a very naughty girl. She simply did that thing that girls do, shrugged and carried on sniffing, very pleased with herself.

The twit went bloody ballistic. I thought he was going to have a heart attack. We went on and finished the search, I got some soap and water and made a very poor job of cleaning up after my mate. The CIB ended up getting commercial cleaners in. The mess was a bit spread out when I had finished.

Two weeks later we were back for another visit. Princess had got over her little tummy problem and was perfectly behaved this time but the owner was foaming at the mouth about us coming in again. The team ignored him and away we went. We never found anything on either search but we enjoyed ourselves immensely.

I was sitting the promotion exams for Sergeant while in the dog section and my feet were getting a bit itchy again.   I transferred back to normal uniform section duties in mid-1979 with the intention of finishing my exams and getting promoted to Sergeant. I was approached by Detective Inspector Jean Dougall to re-join the CIB but I had my heart set on getting promoted. I really appreciated the offer from Jean but I had a few months of study left for my Detective designation and a month-long course to pass as well if I took that route.   This together with my exam study and a young family would have been a big ask. I wanted my stripes. I subsequently worked in the CIB over coming years as an attachment as a Sergeant and on inter-change as a Senior Sergeant, thoroughly enjoying these roles. I never did get around to getting my Detective designation – oh well.

Dyna was allocated to a trainee dog handler but the combination did not work. A decision was made to keep Dyna as a brood bitch and she was given back to me as a family pet which was great.   She continued to live with us until we moved to Whanganui. She had then been released from breeding duties so I gave her to Mum as a pet. She died at the age of ten a very spoiled family pet.

Chapter 15

Then Life stands up and smacks you right between the eyes

Only a person who has had cancer and survived can know the total devastation and sense of loss experienced when the surgeon blithely tells you that the tumour was malignant "but we think we got it all". I was a dog handler based in Newtown when I was diagnosed with testicular cancer at the age of twenty five and the subsequent radiotherapy treatment nearly killed me. I went from eighty four kilos to about seventy kilos in five weeks. I could not eat and Jenny had to put me on a Complan diet. I also insisted on working as I did not want Dyna Dog to become stale. Colin Guppy was a tower of strength at that time. He put me on office duties that allowed me to undertake the daily treatment around the corner at the Wellington Hospital oncology ward.

Jenny and I then had to endure initially two years of uncertainty. At that time testicular cancer did not have the profile it has now. I guess men just died of it. I had a brilliant cancer specialist, Dr Alan Gray, a brother of All Black Ken Gray. Alan quietly explained to Jenny and I that the cure rate for testicular cancer was good. He also explained that any recurrence usually occurred within two years of the operation but that I would have to be under his care for five years to ensure a full clearance. The subsequent year after the operation was awful. Jenny suffered a great deal of stress caring for our daughter Jodie and I as well as working. Coincidentally she was nursing a young guy who was dying of a cancer that originated in a testicle.

Jenny's health suffered for about seven years. If it had not been for her I would never have gone to the doctor in the first place. Cancer does not hurt in the early stages and I only had a lump in my right testicle, nothing to worry about, all the bits worked fine. I would have waited until it began to hurt and probably would have been too late.

Some months after the operation my liver readings played up and I had to have a liver biopsy. A shadow then showed on one lung and we had to spend a horrific week before we found out that the shadow was just that, a faulty x-ray. The liver biopsy was normal but very uncomfortable.

The five years passed and no recurrence occurred. I now have about eight tattoo marks on my body to remind me of those awful days. Cancer patients were tattooed in those days to assist in lining up the radiotherapy machine on the affected areas.

When you are told that you may die of cancer your life completely changes. Things that were important cease to be. Waking up and seeing the sun or walking in the garden becomes more important. The senses of sight and smell become more perceptive. You notice the lovely things in life. I really wondered if I would ever see Jodie grow up. We could not have another child for at least two years as if I died this would only add to Jenny's burden. This explains the almost six year gap between Jodie and our son Luke.

I became paranoid about every cough and lump or spot. I saw cancer lurking everywhere. Personally I found Colin and the guys I worked with extremely supportive. I thrived on survival stories and they all had them. It seemed every cop I worked with knew someone who had cancer and had survived. Those guys really kept me going.

I really got back into sport at about this time, taking up long distance jogging to help me relax and with the thought that a healthy body would fight any cancer off. This has resulted in a lifetime of involvement in endurance type activities. I still swim and cycle albeit not competitively. I began playing club rugby for Wainuiomata again after some years away from the sport, except for social games. I really enjoyed the rugby, playing in the Junior grades with older players nearing the end of their playing days. Good bunch of guys.

Family became far more important to me than before. I was not prepared to chase the jobs or high promotion as some of my peers were doing. When I got sick my one enduring thought was that I wanted to see Jodie grow up. I have managed to achieve this. She is now a forty two year old artist who works with clients with very severe traumatic brain injury. She is a lovely woman, full of life, who still delights in driving her parents to distraction with her alternative ideas on life. Jodie was academically quite able at school and chose Art School after college and then completed a degree in psychology. As parents we would have preferred her to study something that would lead to a more secure life income wise but we are wise enough to let her do her own thing.

I have come not to fear death as such but to recognise its inevitability. I like to think I am a better person because of my brush with cancer. I try to be.

Four years after my surgery Luke arrived. Again another character of a kid. He is now an instructor at the Police College. Luke was a very successful school-boy athlete, gaining national honours in road cycling. He joined the Army after school and spent about 6 years visiting some of the worst trouble sports around the world serving his country. When he left the Army we thought he would settle down to a nice quiet life, but no, he then joined the Police. We are very proud of him.

Bugger me, in March 2008 my GP rang to say that a recent PSA test was slightly up. I trotted along to an urologist who did a biopsy and confirmed prostate cancer. This may have been related to the radiation therapy I had had thirty odd years previously. Due to the damage done by the radiotherapy I could not have surgery so opted for brachytherapy, a procedure where pellets of radioactive material are injected into the prostate, killing the cancer cells. This is only available privately in New Zealand and has proved revolutionary in survival rates for prostate cancer. I have survived thus far but who knows.

Chapter 16

Sergeant—Bit of a change

Being promoted to Sergeant at twenty eight was great. I had been posted back to the Hutt as a Constable a few months after leaving the Dog Section and spent about a year relieving as a Sergeant before completing my last exam in August 1980. The promotion exams in the Police are quite demanding. A lot harder than any university study I have subsequently undertaken.

To be promoted one must pass both education and Police exams in law, evidence, practice and administration. I had been accredited all my education exams to inspector level whilst a Cadet, these being based on my secondary school qualifications.

The great day arrived. On 27th November 1980 I was promoted to Sergeant at Lower Hutt and assigned a section of nine Constables. These guys were a hard case bunch including Ken Laban, Keith Allen, Larry Naik, Mike Arnerich, Harry Reynolds, Paul Feary and Nigel Blackbourn. They were, by and large, motivated and experienced young cops. One or two were inclined to be a bit tired at times but usually rose to the task at hand.

Ken Laban was one of the best cops I ever worked with. A Samoan Kiwi from a very highly respected Wainiomata family, he joined the job a few years after me. I first met Ken when working in Wellington Central. He was in the CIB but eventually found his way to Lower Hutt, starting on my section in early 1981. Ken has been a mate over the years and provided me with great personal support at times. He eventually retired from the Police and has developed a strong political career and also works nationally as a TV broadcaster.

Keith, or antelope as we preferred to call him, was 192 cm of raw energy that we had to channel each day. Keith was a very able and capable copper. Keith spent a year or two in the Hutt then headed off over the hill to Greytown where he was the sole Constable for all of his service. He was also very active in Search and Rescue and the Coastguard.

Harry was an interesting character. He was an ex Royal Ulster Constabulary officer who had left Northern Ireland with his family for a more peaceful life in New Zealand. Harry was a very quiet chap who, when required, always spoke sensibly. He once explained to me that he was losing too many mates in the RUC and suspected his time could be coming. Harry's attitude to policing was relaxed and mature, nothing much worried him. He passed far too young, leaving a young family.

Larry Naik, Mike Arnerich and Nigel Blackbourn were real go-getters. Larry and Mike entered the CIB and Mike is rapidly climbing the ranks. All were great crook catchers as uniform cops.

Paul Feary came onto the section from the Cadets and soon showed he was made of the right stuff. He also joined the CIB.
A great young guy, quiet but with a wicked sense of humour. He and I were to feature in the international press but more of that later.

Section life in the Hutt at this time was excellent. In early 1981 I attended the first Sergeant's Course at the new Royal Zealand Police College at Aotea in Porirua. Members of this course were picked for the ability to march as the College was to be formally opened by Prince Charles and we were expected to parade. Hence the course was made up mainly of ex-Cadets and ex-military personnel.

On the opening day the parade ground was full of courses then attending, including Cadets, Recruits, Sergeants, Senior Constables, Dog Handlers and Commissioned Officers. It was a brilliant occasion and the Prince proved to be a very friendly chap, having lunch and personally talking to many of us. He was quite the little guy.

I spent from November 1980 to December 1981 as a sectional Sergeant in Lower Hutt, leaving the section when I was placed in Prosecutions as a trainee Prosecutor during the enquiry I talk about in the next chapter.

I enjoyed section work and we were a very busy, active, happy little bunch of coppers on my section. In those days in Lower Hutt crime was rife. I encouraged my team to be proactive with street-stops, or in Police jargon of the time "turnovers". This is where Police stop cars moving around at night usually due to minor traffic matters but resulting in talking to the occupants of the vehicles. Many times this resulted in arrests under the Misuse of Drugs Act 1976 or for burglary as well as offences such as driving whilst disqualified or driving under the influence. We were responsible for a very large area and a population of around 160,000 people. On night shift there would only be a Sergeant and up to ten Constables on duty in Lower Hutt and another three or four Constables on duty in Upper Hutt. We were always occupied with attending the local hotels, domestic disputes, sudden deaths, motor accidents with the assistance on the Ministry of Transport, general disorder arising from gang confrontations or fights between groups of youths from different suburbs in the Valley and Wainuiomata, complaints of theft and burglary and any other complaints made by the public.

We had backup if needed from Wellington City Division but they were also a very busy crew most of the time.

Chapter 17

There is nothing funny about this Story.

Many a long serving Police officers has periods in his career that test his resolve. One such time is when the Police subject members to internal enquiries which can result in Court action against one or more Police officers.

Police can be dealt with in the open Court system like any other citizen or by an internal tribunal system under the Police Regulations or both. Penalties under the Tribunal system start at dismissal and work downwards to a fine. The Tribunal is usually a Queen's Counsel and the Police are represented by the Crown Solicitor with the Police member represented by his or her own counsel.

Any internal enquiry looks at criminal liability as well as liability under the Police regulations.

During the Springbok Tour in 1981 I had a very good Constable on my section at the time who, through a momentary lack of control and a later attempt to cover up his actions, received six months' imprisonment. Jack was an excellent Police officer. He was well presented, meticulous in his on-duty behaviour, popular with his colleagues, related well to the public, athletic, and trustworthy. As a measure of the regard he was held in he was stationed at Petone in a position where he would be acting alone for most of his duties. Jack was a very competent young man.

In hindsight, during the last few weeks of the Springbok Tour Jack's behaviour changed. These were very stressful times for most Police and relationship problems were a reasonably common source of concern. The behaviour he exhibited then, and certainly nowadays where stress is readily identified and dealt with, was overlooked by both myself and other older members. We all pretty much had problems of our own at times with the long hours, no time off and enforced absences away from partners and young children. I should perhaps have paid more attention to his behaviour but, not being his normal direct line supervisor, except on night shift, I didn't.

A warning came at a riot at the corner of Rintoul Street and Riddiford Street in Newtown on the day of the Wellington test. We were all in a picket line of about sixty Police trying to prevent about two thousand protestors coming up Rintoul Street to Athletic Park. Jack completely lost his rag and I had to forcibly remove him from the picket line. This was not, in itself, an unusual occurrence, and is one of the reasons Sergeants stand behind a picket line. Removing Constables from a line for a short time after long periods of provocation by protestors is a good safety measure for all concerned. This was not like Jack at all; he had handled much worse provocation than what we were dealing with on that day.

Other symptoms such as being late for duty and the development of a slight disaffection towards his peers and supervisors should have alerted myself and other NCOs, especially Jack's line supervisor, a Sergeant approaching retirement and in a sinecure position. His radar was not working either.

Shortly after the Tour finished Jack and the rest of us stopped a truck full of Black Power gang members in Moera after a long, reasonably slow car chase around most of the Hutt Valley where the occupants of the truck had spent most of their time throwing tools, bricks and other heavy items at the following Police cars. I saw one gang member had assaulted Jack with what I thought in the darkness was a knife. I struck the gang member with my baton, rendering him unconscious and, after ascertaining that Jack was alright and that he had, in fact been struck in a stabbing motion with a crescent spanner, I told Jack to look after the prisoner who we had put in the recovery position, running off to supervise the arrest of several other gang members currently fighting with Police officers.

Unbeknown to me Jack later approached another gang member and assaulted him. This was witnessed by two other Constables who mentioned nothing to me at the time. This gang member had made no overt move to justify the amount of force used.

Later at the Police station, because of the number of arrests made, we undertook a debriefing and when the gang member assaulted by Jack name came up I asked who locked him up. The gang member was at this time at Hutt Hospital with other gang members awaiting treatment. Jack volunteered and I asked the words I would have to try to explain later – "If you can justify the arrest" – meaning was the arrest lawful. Jack agreed and no more was thought of the matter.

About six days later the two Constables who witnessed the assault approached me and told me what had really transpired. This was a Friday evening about a week after the event and I could not have charges against the gang member withdrawn until the following Monday morning. This time delay was to cost me dearly in the months to come. They could not answer when I asked why they had not told me at the de-briefing on the night.

In those days in such a situation the arresting Constable would prepare an information charge sheet against the offender and a report to his supervisor concerning bail recommendations. Usually a week's remand was requested to allow the full prosecution file to be completed, including a summary of the facts of the alleged offence. Later in the week, after the offender had appeared in Court the arresting Constable would then complete the file and send it to the Prosecutor via his Sergeant who would check the file to ensure the charge was sound. On this occasion Jack submitted the file through another Sergeant when we were all on rostered days off, without me seeing it and have the chance to check it. Bearing in mind what happened that night and the high opinion I had of Jack and his work to date I probably would not have queried the arrest at all. Jack's correspondence was always immaculate and Court-ready. He was the least of my problems as far as my sections level of general written correspondence.

An enquiry was started and Jack was eventually suspended from duty. He faced criminal charges in the High Court of attempting to pervert the course of justice and assault. He pleaded guilty and received imprisonment on both charges and the trial judge made the finding that he could not have committed the offences without the collusion of others, namely me!

An extensive enquiry then began into the behaviour of the Police on the night of the arrest, and in particular, my role. The enquiry was conducted by Detective Inspector Colin Lines and was meticulous in every detail. Obviously Jack's family was very concerned about what had happened to him. They were not the only ones. I was disappointed to say the least. At the end of the enquiry I had to face a Police Tribunal to answer several charges under the Police Regulations. I was very ably represented by

John Clapham, later a District Court Judge. I was found guilty of not promptly reporting an offence as I had waited between Friday night and Monday morning to advise the prosecuting Sergeant that the charges against the gang member were malicious and had to be withdrawn. I received the maximum fine of $150.00. My mistake was not organising a special Court sitting to get the charges withdrawn on the Saturday morning.

The enquiry into my behaviour and the subsequent tribunal took most of 1982. I felt very let down and bitter about the way I had been treated. I accept that I should have been aware of the stress Jack was obviously suffering from and done something about it. Perhaps I should have enquired more into the circumstances of the arrest that night. Taken into context mass arrests for riot and disorder were very common in Lower Hutt at that time, and we had just finished that two month rugby tour where mass arrests were the norm. We were, I believe, shell-shocked and numb to a lot of violence by then.

You do trust your experienced and highly competent Constables. Questioning their judgement for every street arrest can lead to problems of morale. If I had uncovered the false arrest that night the result for Jack would likely have been the same – he would have gone to jail for assault. I never saw the prosecution file for the gang member he assaulted, this being prepared by Jack and submitted through another Sergeant.

What sticks in my throat the most is that I started the enquiry that resulted in my own conviction. I was removed from supervisory duties during the enquiry and began work as a Police prosecutor, a job I initially dreaded but came to love. After the enquiry instead of going back to shift duties I elected to remain as a prosecutor.

The Jack affair remained a dark blot on my time in the Police. I learnt a lot, including how zealous senior Police officers can be in undertaking internal enquiries, a job I was to perform myself later in my career. I learned never to really trust anyone of authority in the Police again and distanced myself from most Police after this. Some of my colleagues and peers were of the opinion that I was the reason Jack went to jail. An opinion based on gossip and without knowing the full facts. A few people who I thought were my friends seemed to be unavailable but others were extremely supportive to Jenny and I. Jack made a bad judgement call by assaulting the gang member and then compounded it by falsely charging him with offences he had not committed. These were street offences where the Constable's judgement was usually sufficient to justify the arrest.

Chapter 18

Operation Rugby

Yes, it's that time. Every New Zealand story covering the eighties has to include the Springbok Tour of New Zealand in July to September 1981 and the respective author's version of the events and the Tour's effect on the country.

Being a cop at this time was an interesting experience to say the least. It was amazing that New Zealand's love of rugby could just about bring the country to the brink of anarchy for the sake of another country's reprehensible internal politics. At the time most cops I know loved rugby and could not make the connection between a game they had grown up with and apartheid. I did not know any cop who thought that apartheid was a justifiable policy. I make this observation because over the period of the tour the media and the protest movement were convinced that New Zealand's Police were inherently racist.

The truth was that the Police was required by the oath of office as Constables and the government to enforce the law. The fact that the old grey ones who ran the New Zealand Rugby Football Union in those days and the National government were not going to kowtow to the protest movement had nothing to do with the Police. End of story. It was not the Police role to become embroiled in the whys and wherefores or the politics involved. Our job was to preserve the peace, enforce the country's laws and, where necessary, take action to preserve public safety.

It may be fairer to say that the Muldoon government lent credibility to apartheid by allowing the tour to take place in the first place, knowing that it would plunge the country into mayhem. There was a strong record of opposition in New Zealand to tours by South African sports teams. New Zealand caused a boycott of the 1980 Olympics by most African states because of a policy of not allowing a connection between sport and politics to affect our ongoing sports relationship with South Africa. The National government had a strong track record of telling the protest movement to get stuffed. Various sporting bodies, for the sake of their particular sport, agreed with the government.

The government allowed the tour with full knowledge of the consequences likely to arise. At that time the majority of New Zealanders also wanted the tour to take place because of the love of rugby and the chance to watch the (then) two best rugby-playing nations meet on the field.

Muldoon was also facing re-election in late 1981 and had the cynical foresight to see that the protest movement could alienate the average provincial kiwi. This could result on the left of politics struggling and the country being grateful for a strong government.

Commissioner Walton gave an assurance to the government, when asked, that the Police could manage. In hindsight, it may have been better if he had said we could not. We just about did not. Again it was not Mr Walton's role to advise the government of the error of its ways, but merely to advise the government on the effectiveness of the country's Police. I believe that there was always a determination on behalf of Muldoon that the tour would take place even just to spite the protest movement who was partly comprised of student groups and trade unions, bodies that are an anathema to a National government.

In light of the Police oath the politics of the decision had nothing to do with the Police role. The Police swear to uphold the law and that is what we did, or tried to do. I admit to having no strong feelings about the Springboks coming. I wanted to see the rugby as I love the game. I abhor racism and any system of apartheid. I did not want to see the country I love torn apart. Whilst recognising the right to protest I also recognised the right of the football public to partake in the lawful activity of watching sport.

Thousands of words have been written about the tour by people far more learned than me. My view of the tour was first hand and not protected by the benefit of hindsight from a lounge chair or an academic discussion group. The reality is that thousands of New Zealanders, mostly normal decent law abiding people, mobilised for a cause they thought dearly about, taking them, in many cases, into direct conflict with the Police for the first time in their lives. Thousands of Police had to face neighbours, family and friends.

The tour took me to just about every town where a game was played. We worked twelve hour shifts in our home stations when not travelling with no leave or days off allowed. This continued for the eight weeks of the tour. Two thousand Police out of a force of four thousand were deployed at the third test in Auckland.

After over thirty-five years it is difficult to remember the exact details of the logistics involved. My memories are of working long hours, being scared stiff at times, being bored most of the time when away from home, and being astonished at the violence exhibited by people involved in both sides of the tour. At the first game in Gisborne my section and I were required to work night shifts. The Springbok team were staying at a hotel in Gladstone Road. The local anti-tour group's favourite tactic was to attack the hotel at night making as much noise as possible to disrupt the activities of the team.

We would deploy to the hotel and drive the protestors away, possibly arresting a few. On one occasion I attempted to stop a van-load of protestors as they were leaving. The van hit me, throwing me over a nearby Police car. I was shocked but not seriously hurt. The university student driving the van had never been in trouble with the Police. She was subsequently charged with dangerous driving causing injury and convicted.

I suffered a hip injury which, although minor at the time, resulted in me having a bilateral hip replacement over twenty years later.

No matter how careful one is things can still go belly-up

While working in Gisborne I was in a Group of cops from Wellington and Lower Hutt, most of whom I knew and many of whom were good friends. As I said above we were all put on night shift looking after the game venue and the Springbok team accommodation as the protest movement was in town and very well-organised.

After our first night several of the group approached myself and John Hood, a fellow sergeant from Lower Hutt, asking about a trip to a winery in the morning after we knocked off. In those days there were several very good wineries near Gisborne. John and I checked with our Inspector and agreed to accompany a van load of off duty cops to a winery. They were to go in plainclothes and to have breakfast before we left, being back in time for lunch and then to bed for further duty that night. All good.

After breakfast the following morning about fifteen of us set off for a winery in a van driven by a local Constable from the Logistics section who was to be our guide. We tasted some wine and some members bought bottles to take home with them and their families in Wellington. At about 11.30 we all got back in the van to head back to the Police base for lunch as arranged. At about this time I noticed one guy who was making a nuisance of himself, picking arguments and basically being a dick. I asked one of the Wellington guys who he was and he said he did not know him.

By the time we had got back to the motels where our Police base and mess was this guy was out of control in the back of the van, abusive and threatening. He was in danger of getting a slap from one of the team when John and I intervened, sent the crew off to lunch and stayed in the van with this cop who no one knew. We asked him where he was staying and he told us the name of a motel. We asked the driver to take us there as we intended to put him to bed. It was clear that he was heavily intoxicated. He was not having a bar of this and started throwing punches at John and myself.

We were a bit shocked to say the least. Our plan to keep his behaviour quiet went out the window when a local Senior Sergeant approached the van in a very aggressive way demanding to know what we were doing. We tried to explain to him that the cop was not well, but appeared to be heavily intoxicated. He accused us of being drunk and disorderly, a bit stiff as neither of us had much to drink at all due to being in charge of the group of off-duty cops. We were also off duty and in our own time.

This scenario played out in front of hundreds of off duty and on duty Police coming and going at the motel for lunch. John and I tried to reason with the Senior Sergeant but he was having none of this, shouting at us and ordering us out of the van. He then ordered two off-duty Senior Sergeants to take us into custody at PR24 baton point. John and I were absolutely stunned but then recovered enough to demand what we were being arrested for. He would not reply. The other Seniors appeared to be quite embarrassed. To settle things we walked off with them to a nearby office where the twat of a Senior Sergeant locked us in a room. Meanwhile the drunk or sick cop ran off!

Once John and I recovered enough to realise we had not actually been arrested for anything we left the office, telling the staff we were going back to our motel if their boss wanted to see us. He had, by then disappeared. I must admit things did get a bit shouty between the Senior Sergeant and John and me but we committed no offences that I was aware of.

The cop we were trying to look after ran off to a nearby dairy where he collapsed on the floor. The owner called an ambulance. When this arrived the cop punched the ambos. They called the local Police who arrived and were also punched by the cop. He was then arrested and taken into custody.

When he was searched at the station they found his Police ID card, realising he was a cop. He was then put into a detox unit and flown back to Wellington the following day. The back story to this clown was that he was an alcoholic who had been transferred from a small station to Wellington the previous week under supervision. He was a very ill man but no one in management sought fit to keep him off the tour or to advise supervisors of his issues. I believe he eventually got the help he needed and recovered. I hope so for his sake. I do not to this day know his name, nor has he approached either John or I to apologise.

Anyway the Senior Sergeant in Gisborne, a well reputed "Fitter", reported John and I to the Commissioner for a series of criminal and Police regulation offences including assault and insubordination. A "Fitter" in Police jargon is a cop, usually an NCO or Officer, who takes great delight in prosecuting other police for allegations under the criminal law or the Police disciplinary law. These weirdos are thankfully few and far between but their behaviour says a lot about their make-up. They can be very dangerous individuals, usually despised and feared by all ranks. They seem to suffer from a God-Complex.

Once John and I realised we were being reported for the incident in the car park of the motel we decided to run our own enquiry in parallel but separate from the Commissioner's enquiry. We had been approached by many staff to say that they had witnessed this clown's behaviour towards us. A very good mate, a Sergeant in Wellington Central, acquired a copy of the inquiry file, left somewhere by a sympathetic commissioned officer. He then arranged for cops from all around New Zealand, unknown to each other, to provide job sheets outlining their observations that morning.

We presented our enquiry file to the Commissioner via Bob Moodie, the president of the NZ Police Association. The upshot of all this kerfuffle was that the Commissioner would take no action against either of us, that we should have been made aware of the cop's health issues and that there was basically nothing in the allegations made by the Senior Sergeant of Assault or any other offence. It was suggested to us that we write to the Senior Sergeant expressing regret about the incident as he was a very hard-working and dedicated officer who thought he was doing the right thing (weren't we all). John refused. I wrote to him a Clayton's apology, simply that I regretted ever meeting him.

This man went on to achieve higher rank but was feared and despised by most who knew him.

More Mayhem

The next stop on the tour was the Waikato game in Hamilton on 25th July 1981. History has recorded the events of the game that never was. I believe the Commissioner had prior knowledge that protestors were to invade the pitch and kept staff at a minimum with maximum reserves. I was on reserve at the Hamilton Police station with my section, five Detectives from Auckland placed in uniform for the tour. They were great guys. We had an Inspector from Headquarters in charge of us who no one knew. The seven of us escorted two thousand protestors from Hamilton City to Rugby Park. We actually drove in two cars at the back of the march.

Upon arrival at the park the march did a left wheel at the northern perimeter, shouldered aside the few young cops standing there and simply walked onto the ground. We raced from the car and, with about twenty other cops split the march so that only a few hundred got onto the ground. It was the most frightening moment of my life. We were outnumbered hundreds to one and the protesters were very unhappy.

The relief I felt when a line of what seemed to be hundreds of cops from Wellington slammed through the marchers to relieve us was overwhelming. They had just arrived at the ground and were in reserve when the invasion occurred.

We formed a human wall chained together by our belts to hold the fence line. Rugby supporters were throwing cans into the crowd, they were taking our short batons out of our pockets and assaulting protestors who were within reach. We were on a bank above the marchers and, every now and then, a cop would slip down the bank. A brawl would ensue when his colleagues retrieved him. I believe to this day that we would have lost a guy if we had not used the maximum force available to save these fellows.

I noted then Government MP Marilyn Waring and later MP Donna Awatere in the thick of the crowd urging people to attack our line. Dear old women just like Mum were flicking sand into our eyes and calling us murderers and butchers. I never did work that one out! These were very emotional times.

After the game was called off we had to escort the marchers back to Hamilton City as, needless to say, the rugby watching fraternity were less than pleased that their game did not eventuate. There were very real concerns for the personal safety of the protestors. The people who had just spent some two hours assaulting us, spitting at us, abusing us and flicking sand into our eyes now relied on us to protect them from the objects of their hatred, the rugby watching public.

We did our job and duly escorted them back into town. My section was right at the front of the march. In the main street of Hamilton a young man approached the lead marchers and drop kicked one in the head. Paul Doggett and I arrested him for assault with intent to injure and the bloody marchers cheered us. I have seen photos of this incident and it took me a while to identify the cops concerned. We all looked scared out of our wits.

On that day I was, for the only time in my career, ashamed of being a cop. We had been let down by the administration who, I believe, knew darn well what the marchers intended. It was lucky no one was killed, either cop or marcher, as a result. I attended a meeting at the Hamilton Police station that night to witness a vote of no-confidence in the Commissioner, proposed by Ross Meurant, then a Senior Sergeant on Red Squad. I have subsequently reconsidered Bob Walton's position. He was a good Commissioner and an experienced leader, both in the Army and the Police. I like to think that he was trying to give Muldoon a message, call off the tour as we cannot cope.

An interesting side issue arose when I met my half-brother Peter. Peter was, in 1981 a journalist for the Auckland Star and Rex, my other half-brother, was a photographer on the same paper. Both were amongst the media contingent at Hamilton and were at the hole in the fence with the protestors. Peter believes that Rex would have photos of me in the line. Really weird. I had not met Peter or Rex at that time. They were from my father's first marriage which ended in about 1950. I grew up knowing of them but having no contact at all until I was an adult. They are both great guys who now live in Australia.

After this game I returned home to normal duties. In total I also travelled to Nelson, got to see the game there as I was on the pitch. We were ordered to face the crowd and not the game but we just disobeyed the order. Dunedin, - flew from Wellington in the morning and sat in a bus all day and flew home again. Christchurch, again sat in a bus on reserve outside McAllister Park and then flew home again. Whangerei, sat in a hall and watched television on Reserve.

The New Zealand Maori Game

On the 25th August 1981 I flew to Napier with my own section of Lower Hutt cops for the game against the New Zealand Maoris at McLean Park. Most of my section were Maori, Polynesian or Indian with Harry Reynolds and I being the only white boys. The protestors were out in force but were, overall, very good-natured. However they used some great tactics to try to give the Police a hard time. They were particularly scathing of the brown cops in Napier, targeting them for special abuse, calling them "Uncle Toms" and "Potatoes". My guys just laughed at them and carried on making jokes with the closest protestors.

The protest movement decided to have a wee march around the streets surrounding McLean Park. At every intersection the march would split, making us split our escort. They seemed to forget that we were there to actually protect them from some very pissed off rugby fans who, by then, had had a gutsful of their antics. Every time they halved the march they also halved our ability to protect them. Most of our part of the march were very good-natured well-meaning people but they still liked to give us a hard time. By the time we had finished the march there was only me and one of the guys left to look after about fifty protestors. Not much good if some nasty rugby types decided to start belting a few of them. The game went on anyway. I missed it of course but the Maori All blacks held the Boks to a twelve all draw which was a credit to the selectors.

The Royal New Zealand Air Force flew us everywhere in their slow old Hercules, Andovers and a 727 usually reserved for VIPs. We always seemed to get the Hercules when we were far from home and very tired. They are great planes but not very fast and horrendously noisy.

I also worked at the two games held in Wellington. I was involved in most of the protest activity in Wellington, helping to lock up about fifty protestors at Horokiwi when they tried to block the Hutt Motorway. The Scene Commander took to the hills when his second-in-charge, Senior Sergeant Noel Wynne, suggested commandeering an Eastbourne bus. Noel did it without his blessing and all the marchers and cops piled onto the bus for a drive back to the Hutt station leaving the few bemused passengers to get lifts elsewhere.

A thing that struck me during the tour was the lack of command ability portrayed by a few Commissioned Officers. There were, of course, many excellent officers, but a few found the whole deal too much to handle. They were simply out of their depth, trying to lead men and women who were, basically, far more street-wise. As an NCO I sometimes found that orders were not given quick enough, leading Senior Sergeants and, on occasions, Sergeants, to make decisions they did not have the rank to make.

At the other end of the rank spectrum most Constables performed admirably. I had reason on one or two occasions to remove some of the more emotionally-charged Constables from the lines fearing they would completely lose it, but that was my job as a section leader.

Whilst the tour was the biggest Policing operation of the 20th century it had its fun times. Work was distressing and, at times, downright frightening. Off duty I managed to catch up with a lot of old mates from Trentham days. We all got to see a lot of New Zealand and live in some of the nicest pubs on offer.

The tour ground to its ultimate climax in Auckland on the day of the third test. I missed this, having to work in Wellington at demos. I am glad I missed it as this was the closest New Zealand had got to a complete breakdown of law and order. Colleagues who were there described it as war. Everybody got on the bandwagon to attack the Police. Gangs, students, criminals, all decided to have a field day.

After the tour finished there were months of Court cases and enquiries to endure. I was glad I was there, but I was happy when it was over.

Our son Luke was born a month before the Tour started. Whilst I was away Jenny had to keep the home fires burning. Like most Police families we found the Tour took its toll on family life. Just the worry of a husband, wife, father or mother being away at demos that were nightly broadcast on TV was more than enough for some families. Jenny carried on as she has always done, looking after a new baby and little daughter on her own. My family lived nearby and Mum was always there to help. We never really experienced the problems some Police families did with other family members or neighbours who held opposing views. Living in Wainuiomata probably helped. Most of our neighbours were working people who loved sport and could not make the connection between rugby and apartheid. They were also mainly quite pro-Police.

Chapter 19

Before the Bench

In early 1982 I began work as a full time Police prosecutor at the Lower Hutt District Court. I was offered this option rather than possible suspension while a serious enquiry was undertaken into my actions concerning a cop Jack who was jailed for assault and perverting the course of justice.

I decided to take the job offer as sitting all day at home and getting under Jenny's feet would not have been helpful. The enquiry and subsequent tribunal took thirteen months. In that time I gained the basics of prosecuting under the gentle tutelage of Senior Sergeant Bryan Courtenay and Sergeant Bob Bull. The Police decided not to send me on a prosecutor's course as this could be a waste of time and money if it all went bad for me in the enquiry. Oh ye of little faith.

I thoroughly enjoyed the role and working with Court staff and members of the local Law Society. A Prosecutor's role is to present the evidence for the Police or the Crown in a fair and unbiased way to the court. It is also to ensure that all evidence offered by the defence is tested in court, also in a fair and unbiased way. The prosecutor has to operate within the rules of evidence and disclosure at all times and to maintain professional relationships with all parties to any hearing including other Police, lawyers, defendant and court staff. The prosecutor has the added duty of advising the judge or the Police of any concerns about the actions of police members involved in a case.

Lower Hutt District Court was a very busy place in the 1980s with courts sitting every day and using at least two, sometimes three full time prosecutors. Mondays and Tuesdays were list days and Children Court days.   Sentencing (or prize-giving) took place most days but especially on Tuesday afternoons when the great unwashed would turn up with their suitcases and/or toothbrushes planning a short, or sometimes not so short, holiday on the State.

In those days we also prosecuted deposition hearings or lower Court hearings prior to charges being referred to a District Court or High Court jury trial.   These hearings could take days due to the complexity of evidence needed to create a case that could be put before a jury.

I also prosecuted defended hearings in the District Court, learning to lead evidence for witnesses and to cross-examine and re-examine witnesses.   These hearings could take from an hour to several days as well, depending on the number of witnesses to be called by the Police and the defence.

The defence was usually undertaken by lawyers but on occasions a defendant would undertake his own defence – a very risky idea. There is a very true saying among the legal fraternity and the Bench – *A person who defends himself has a fool for a client.*
Most District Court Judges were helpful to both the defence counsel and the Police Prosecutor, but not all.   Some Judges enjoyed humiliating others while on the bench.   To be fair they were usually as hard on lawyers as they were on Police prosecutors.

The prosecutors also acted as Police representatives at Coroner's Court, leading all the evidence into the circumstances of deaths reported to the Coroner.

I was eventually cleared in the Jack enquiry but chose to remain as a prosecutor. I enjoyed the day to day interaction with Court staff and mostly young lawyers. I know a lot of Police do not have much time for the legal profession but I found great friendships with a lot of lawyers that I enjoy to this day. Yes, they had their funny ways, but so did the Police. As people they were warm, very bright and fun to be with either at work or away from work.

There were difficult and treacherous lawyers, but I knew them and adopted my dealings accordingly. I could be just as difficult if needed. Whilst they behaved like this to the Police they also tended to behave similarly to their fellow members of the Bar.
In early 1983 when Jen and I moved to Whanganui the local Law Society held a farewell for us, providing me with a very nice farewell present. I felt very touched and privileged.

After a short time running a small section of cops in Whanganui I again became a full time sole prosecutor in the Whanganui District Court for Judges Bill Unwin and Derek Lowe. Whanganui was a much quieter court but I was just as busy as I had been in Lower Hutt. Again the majority of the local Law Society and the Court staff were excellent to deal with and to work with. I worked in this position for two years before going to other duties in the CIB and then further promotion.

During this time Judge Unwin asked me on several occasions to consider studying for the Bar. I took these comments as compliments for my ability as a Prosecutor but told His Honour that I had a young family and would have to shift to Auckland or Wellington to attend Law School. I also had to make a living. I could have asked the Police for study leave and assistance but knew that this would not be forthcoming after the "Jack Affair". In those days it took the Police a couple of years to forgive and forget after a cop had been in front of a Tribunal. Also we loved living in Whanganui and did not want to leave.

Peter Brosnahan, a class-mate from St Bernard's College, practices as a barrister in Whanganui so him and I shared some time together in court at times on opposite sides of the fence. We were old school-mates outside of court, all business in court. I remained a part time prosecutor until I left the Police in 1992. It was part of Police work I thoroughly enjoyed.

Chapter 20
Whakapohane

One of the fairy tale romances of the 20th century was the wedding of Prince Charles and Lady Diana Spencer in 1981. In early 1983 news reached the Police that the Royal couple was to tour New Zealand in April. As with any Royal Tour a massive security operation was mounted. This would be the first large operation the Police carried out on a national basis since the Springbok Tour. It was a very well-planned operation and I was involved in various aspects of the tour as a Sergeant with a section of Hutt Constables. We travelled to various parts of the country and it was a very enjoyable time both for the young couple and for their minders. They were very popular, the young princess especially so.

Royal Tours have always been big affairs as far as the Police are concerned and this was no exception. With the rugby tour still fresh in everyone's minds the Police wanted to show the country and the World that we could do a good job.

On Wednesday, 20th April 1983 the Prince and Princess were due to fly into Wellington airport. We were to be deployed around the airport in a loose cordon to ensure nothing untoward happened. With Royal Tours the main task is crowd control but also balanced with the wish of the public to see the VIP. At the briefing prior to the landing we were told by Inspector Whiro Ratahi that a well-known Maori activist Nathan Dun Mihaka, or Te Ringu Mangu Mihaka, was planning to perform the Maori act of Whakapohane in front of the Royal couple. Whakapohane is the act of showing disdain or contempt for someone and is simply turning and baring the backside to the person to be insulted. Whiro stressed the need for some sensitivity if Dun did his whakapohane.

After the briefing I was sent to the corner of Calabar Road and Broadway, opposite the airport. My section of Constables, together with other Lower Hutt cops, were spread along the road. The nearest cop to me was Paul Feary.

As the Royal motorcade approached from our left our attention was diverted to a male Maori dressed in a piupiu or grass skirt, dancing out of Broadway towards Calabar Road. It became clear that this was to be the Whakapohane incident referred to in the briefing. I knew Dun Mihaka from previous encounters and recognised him. Paul and I ran to Mihaka and arrested him, placing him on the ground in Calabar Road. He did not resist and the arrest was quite passive. He was handcuffed and taken to a nearby van. In the meantime his partner Diana Prince attacked a couple of the cops assisting with her placard stick and was also arrested. The incident was over in about two minutes and I did not think many people saw it. The only people who saw what had happened other than the watching Police and Mihaka's supporter's were the international press entourage unfortunately.

Mihaka, Paul and I had our photos spread around the world within twelve hours. It was the biggest incident of the Tour with questions being asked about how "dangerous natives" can be allowed to approach so closely to the Royals.

Mihaka duly pleaded not guilty and he and his wife had their day (or days) in Court. From memory I think he was convicted of disorderly or offensive behaviour. He later published a book, sending me a copy. Dun is a character and knows how to maximise publicity for the cause of Maori sovereignty. We got on well at the time. Paul and I babysat their kiddies in the Court waiting room while they were giving evidence.

In late 2015 I was visiting an elderly Maori client of mine in Otaki. Another elderly gentleman was also at the hui. My client talked to me about knowing what I got up to when Princess Diana was here thirty two years previously. I was not sure what he meant until I looked again at the other elderly chap and realised that it was Dun.

My client is and has always been an activist for Maori sovereignty and I always enjoyed our chats. Obviously with this background he knew Dun who also lives in Otaki now. We all had a great korero.

The interesting thing about Dun's trial was him summonsing Whiro Ratahi to give evidence for the defence about the briefing and the meaning of Whakapohane. Whiro was a great cop and is a great guy. He gave good evidence of the cultural significance of what Dun had done and how he took pains to explain this to Paul and me following the arrest. Paul and I, both being of Maori descent, had no real problems with this and we ensured the correct charge was laid.

It was my first encounter with the effect of Tikanga Maori on the court process. At that time it was quite common for protestors, whatever their cause, to summons Police to give evidence for the defence in order to shows cracks in Police procedure and the prosecution case. The Police members concerned have no choice but to answer the summons and be grilled by the defendants.

I guess everyone gets to be famous at least once in their lifetime. Paul and I ended up on the front pages of a lot of the world's newspapers arresting Dun and his partner Diana. We then sunk thankfully back into oblivion.

We carried on around the country looking after the princess and her errant husband with no further disruption to what was a very happy time for New Zealand after the dark days of the Springbok Tour. It was nice to face crowds who actually were not insulting us or throwing sand and other small items at us.

Chapter 21

Pegleg – A Tragedy

John Edward Morgan grew up in a normal family in Naenae during the 1950's and 60's. He was about my age but we did not know each other, him living some distance away from me. I knew of him as a teenager and knew to keep away from him. He was regarded, even as a teenager, as a very dangerous individual to cross.

Morgan began offending at a young age and was a hardened petty criminal by the time he was twenty one. He was quick to violence and ruthless in his dealings with others. He was a slight chap but he just seemed to be wired wrong. His parents and other family were lovely people and must have worried about him a lot.

At some stage in his young life he lost a lower leg in a motor accident and became known as "Pegleg" by all who knew him, but not to his face.

As a young cop in the Hutt in the early 1970s I did not have much, if anything to do with Morgan. He was, by then, a regular attendee in the CIB office at Lower Hutt Police station as suspect in burglaries and other crime in the Hutt Valley.

I would, in the early 1980's when stationed back in Lower Hutt, run into Morgan when patrolling the pubs around town and would turn him over as we did with all well-known criminals out and about at night. He was usually just surly but co-operative. Never a man to have a joke with or to pass the time of day as we did a lot with other very bad boys we spoke to. These guys expected to be stopped and spoken to by us, just normal business to them and most enjoyed a chat with the pigs.

Sometime in the early 1980's Morgan was serving time in what is now Rimutaka Prison, then known as Witako Prison, near Upper Hutt. He had received information from a criminal associate that his then partner was having an affair. Morgan escaped from prison with the intention of murdering his partner. We had information that he had access to firearms and we knew, due to his personality, that he would not hesitate to shoot his partner or anyone who got in his way. Morgan was regarded by us as extremely dangerous.

The CIB staff moved his partner to a safe house and set up an operation to stake out his partner's home in a quiet suburban street in Taita. The plan was that two armed cops would sit in the house on shifts in case Morgan turned up. The operation was run for a week or so with no luck. I did a couple of shifts sitting in the dark all night with a revolver and a mate for company. We were in radio contact with the operations base in the Lower Hutt Police station and assistance was not far away. I am not sure whether Morgan got wind of us or not, but one crew thought he turned up one night, checked around the outside of the property and left.

The operation was wound down after a week or so and we waited for events to take their course. Morgan's partner was safe so we really just needed to wait until he popped his head up, knowing that this would happen sooner or later.

We received information from someone living nearby that Morgan had been seen going into the house a few days later. We slowly and quietly evacuated all the nearby houses and mobilized the Armed Offenders Squad who tear-gassed the house. Morgan, who had been hiding in the attic, fell through the particle board ceiling fighting mad. He was eventually arrested after a struggle and was taken into custody. Morgan went back to prison to finish his term plus a few extra months for escaping and other charges arising from his time out.

Upon his release from prison Morgan continued his criminal ways until the day before Xmas Eve 1982. That night he and some associates visited the Sunset Disco, a night club in Wellington. Either on the way into the night club or on the way out after being evicted Morgan stabbed a young twenty four year old man, Sinclair Inglis, without provocation, killing him instantly in the club. The victim was unknown to Morgan and had not spoken to him, just walking past minding his own business. There had been an altercation in the club and I guess Morgan just felt he had to take his temper out on someone and the victim was in the wrong place at the wrong time.

Morgan was positively identified by patrons and staff at the club as the person responsible for the killing. He had left prior to the Police arriving so a search was mounted for him, especially in the Hutt Valley, his normal haunt.

The following day, Xmas Eve, was, as expected, a very busy day on the streets around Lower Hutt with everybody out shopping and getting ready for Xmas celebrations. I was Acting Senior Sergeant for the day, responsible for running any operations that occurred during my shift.

We had patrols out looking for Morgan and in the early afternoon one of these patrols visited the Silverstream tip in case Morgan may be getting rid of evidence. Sure enough, they saw Morgan at the tip alone, driving a roofless Landrover vehicle. The crew tried to stop Morgan but he took off out onto the main road, hitting the Police car on the way and headed back towards Taita through the Taita Gorge.

By this time I was mounting an operation to get more staff on the road, set up road blocks, contact a helicopter to get in the air so we could follow Morgan and call out the Armed Offender Squad (AOS) and dog section.

Morgan drove his Landrover at moderate speed all the way down the Eastern Hutt Road towards Naenae shops where he clipped a car driven by a woman out shopping, wrecking the car. He carried on and several attempts by Police to stop him resulted in him ramming the Police cars, knocking them out of contention as well. Morgan drove on down Cambridge Terrace and on to Whites Line followed by several Police vehicles in a pursuit. Due to the Landrover's mechanical condition the pursuit was not overly fast but still very dangerous due to the traffic conditions that day. No thought was given to abandoning the chase as we did not have helicopter surveillance until Morgan got into Wainuiomata and Morgan had already killed once and had no intention of giving himself up to the Police.

Morgan drove over the Wainiuiomata Hill and down the main road onto the Coast Road leading to the sea. This is an isolated farming area with minimal traffic. By this time a dog handler and dog had arrived overhead in a helicopter. Morgan turned onto a farm paddock and crossed a stream with his Landrover, resulting in the following Police being unable to follow in their two wheel drive cars.

The crossing caused the Landrover to stop for some reason and at that point the helicopter landed near Morgan. The dog handler got out with his dog and called on Morgan to surrender several times. Morgan was brandishing an axe and was about five metres away from the handler. Morgan threw the axe at the handler hitting him in the head. At the same time the handler shot Morgan in the foot with his issue Police .38. Morgan was still mobile and was shot immediately again by another Police member nearby, dropping to the ground.

The handler was very seriously injured and was rushed to hospital with severe head injuries. He was off duty for many months and made a slow recovery, eventually returning to full duties.

Obviously First Aid was administered to Morgan at the scene but he had died almost instantly after being shot.

The normal enquiries started after the shooting and the Police Officers were eventually found to be justified in shooting Morgan. The criminal enquiry into the stabbing also became a coronial enquiry and it was established without doubt that Morgan was the person responsible for stabbing the young man to death the previous night in Wellington.

The fallout from this shooting was interesting. Everybody in the criminal element in Naenae had an opinion of course. We were advised to keep our presence low-key in the area for a couple of weeks and to try to engage people in conversation about what had actually happened when we did visit the area. This was difficult of course as there were still at least two enquiries running following the murder and the shooting.

The average low life criminal in Naenae has no love for the Police so we were never going to be able to explain what had happened satisfactorily. I personally did not bother. I knew most of these guys and they were just petty criminals or associates who probably feared and hated Morgan but it gave them a chance to have a go at the Police. I just carried on dealing with them as I always had.

Morgan's family was, rightly, devastated by what had happened to him and it is perhaps understandable if they still harbour resentment towards the Police over the shooting.

However there was also another family, the Inglis, who had lost a young son and brother for no other reason than the bad-temper of an unbalanced, vicious and cold-blooded criminal.

I know which family I feel the most for but there were no winners out of this tragedy. Morgan was the author of his own demise in threatening the dog handler with the axe. The handler did not have time to release his dog or to withdraw. The handler still has the scars from that day.

During the course of my time in the Police there were numerous Police shootings, members having to take a person's life due to an immediate danger to the Police present or to another person or member of the public. The fallout from shooting someone can be very difficult for the Police Officer concerned. Police are trained in the use of firearms and Armed Offender Squad members have very intense training in firearm use, tactics and procedures. Police are not soldiers and have to operate within the law and policy of the time. The statutory boundaries for shooting a person in New Zealand are legally very tight, as they should be. There must be an immediate danger to life and no other option available to preserve the life of another.

I know several retired Police who have shot people in the course of their duty and it marks every single one of those men in some way. Police are not trained to be killers as soldiers are but they still have to make instant and accountable decisions to perhaps kill another person to preserve life. They then have to face at least two enquiries, one being a homicide investigation and the other being an enquiry from the Independent Police Conduct Authority. Both these investigations will be thorough and scrupulous. They will also have to put up with the opinions of the media and every Tom Dick and Harry who is an instant armchair expert on what should have happened and how they would have dealt with the offender by shooting the weapon out of his hand for example.

Nowadays Police who shoot suspects have access to decent counselling and are, generally, very well cared for. Their anonymity is still preserved no matter what and I hope this continues but it worries me that great efforts are made by certain pressure groups and the media to have Police who shoot identified. Some Police find this all too much and, for their own sake and the sake of their families, they leave the Police to begin an anonymous life.

I have been placed in the "shoot, don't shoot" situation a couple times as a member of the AOS but thankfully the moment passed in each situation and the offender survived to usually go on and offend another day.

I acknowledge reference to "Wellington – the Dark Side" pp 17 and 18 – William Minchin

Chapter 22

A new start for us all

For various reasons, both career-wise and personal we decided that we would seek a transfer away from Wellington in early 1983. I was settled happily as a prosecutor in the Hutt, a very busy Court, but various issues in my extended family were impacting on our lives too much. I am, by nature, a family guy, choosing family as the priority over advancement in any work I have ever done, but too much family can be overwhelming. Jenny and I needed a change for our own little family's sake.

Shifting to Whanganui was and has been very good for us as a family. It was also very good for my career. I took over a shift of three or four Constables in Whanganui for a couple of years and I had the opportunity to attend more advanced course at the Police College and also began studying for the Senior Sergeant exams. Since being placed in prosecutions in Lower Hutt my career had taken a swing upwards despite the various enquiries that bedevil active career cops at times. I tended to spend about six to eight weeks of every year between 1983 and 1992 at the Police College as a student on courses, or later as an instructor on AOS Qualifying courses.

The District Commander in Whanganui at the time was Superintendent Brian Dean. He was a close friend of my old boss, the Divisional Commander in Lower Hutt, Superintendent Jim Maguire. Jim had briefed Brian about me and the Jack affair, obviously including my general competence as a Sergeant. Brian welcomed me with open arms, saying that he had heard good things about me and that he expected to continue to see these from then on. We got on famously. Brian like Jim was a great boss, some in Whanganui not knowing how good he was.

Being a sectional Sergeant again was great for a change even if the five week roster of shift work was hard on the body. With only three or four Constables to look after I found time on my hands so used to get the crew to be more proactive in their policing, encouraging turnovers during the hours of darkness. This resulted again in an increase in arrests for crimes and dishonesty and drug offending.

What struck me on arriving in Whanganui was an acceptance from a lot of Uniform Branch staff that the three patched gangs in town, the Black Power, the Galgoffa bike gang (now Hells Angels) and the Mongrel Mob could ride roughshod over the police if they chose to. Some of the troops, including one or two Sergeants, felt that this was not right and we decided that we would stop taking crap from these losers and show them who actually was in charge of the town in terms of crime. In my first week on night shift we approached a group of Black Power in cars on the street. They had been giving some uniform Police a hard time and nothing was happening. I spoke to the driver of one of the cars, Tui Kuru, the President of the chapter. He gave me some mouth so I asked him to get out of the car. He told me to fuck off. I then opened the driver's door and dragged him out of the car onto the ground, kneeling on him, arresting him for obscene language in a public place. This caused his mates to get out and act staunch towards the Police, menacing them and threatening physical violence. I ordered the staff present to begin locking these clowns up for breaching the peace. Some stood around not knowing what to do but thankfully a few cops started getting into the spirit of the moment. Things progressed and most were arrested for substantive street offending such as threatening behaviour, assault on police, resisting arrest etc. We filled the cells with smelly fat gang members that night and told them a few hours later when they were bailed that the same would be happening again very soon.

I was a bit worried about how this would pan out with the bosses but I need not have worried. They were pleased that they had another Sergeant in town with some balls. One of the Senior Sergeants was actually at the scene watching when we arrested the gang but did not interfere, something I appreciated but also worried a bit about as I did not know him that well. He later told me he just wanted to see how I would handle the situation and how my actions would affect the other Police standing around and watching.

Whanganui was a bit of an old man's home in terms of Sergeants and Senior Constables in those days so a lot of younger, keen staff simply did not have the direction they wanted and needed to become effective street cops. This had become a source of concern for the senior administration. The significant thing about this was the Sergeants who wanted to sort the town out were all ex-Cadets who had spent years working in the large cities with most of us having worked on Team Policing Units. We were used to mass arrest situations and gang confrontations. We were all quite young, late twenties and early thirties, so were all physically very fit and very motivated, making good examples for young Constables to follow.

Many of the troops in Whanganui came direct from the Police College upon graduation and had simply not been shown how to deal with gangs on the street. Once they got it they were fine and the gangs started spending a lot of time in our company and a lot of money and time at Court. The gangs in Whanganui were quite soft compared to the animals I had been dealing with in the Hutt.

At the time the Whanganui Criminal Investigation Branch (CIB) office was run by a grizzled old Detective Senior Sergeant, Rob Butler. He was a great guy and had a very experienced team of detectives. Rob learned that I had spent some time in the CIB in Wellington and wanted me to join his office as a Detective Sergeant. I had to explain to Rob that I had not qualified as a Detective but he would not allow this to be an issue. He wanted a fourth Detective Sergeant for some reason and none of his Detectives were qualified for promotion at the time. I demurred as I could see the issues arising in a small office if an unqualified Detective Sergeant was appointed.

In early 1985 I took over the Prosecutor's job in Whanganui, doing this full time for about two years. I then moved "upstairs" in early 1987, taking over the Uniform Branch Enquiry office under the control of the officer in charge of the CIB, Detective Senior Sergeant Peter Scott. Peter is an old friend from Lower Hutt. He spent most of his career in the CIB retiring as a Detective Senior Sergeant in Wanganui. Peter is great guy and a brilliant sportsman. We share many memories.

I first worked with Peter in Lower Hutt. We were young Detective Constables in 1976 when the World Softball Championships were held in Lower Hutt. South Africa sent a team to the champs. Obviously this attracted the attention of the protest movement who picketed the team's accommodation at the Grove Motels in Lower Hutt city. The Police provided the team with around the clock security at the motel. Pete and I looked after the whole team for one very wet Wellington day when they could not play. I am not sure what we could do as they were all bigger than me and a lot were bigger than Pete. I am sure they could look after themselves just fine. Being a wet day the very small group of protestors had decided to go home as well.

When I started working for Scotty in 1987 it soon became apparent that street crime was rife in Whanganui at the time and that it needed an intense concentration of resources for a year or so to curb it. At that time the Police operated Crime Control Units which were CIB based squads of both detectives and plainclothes Constables under the direction of a Detective Sergeant or Uniform Sergeant with CIB experience. These were normally operated in the large cities but Scotty wanted one. He was not allowed to call it a Crime Control Unit for obscure political reasons so he penned the name Special Tactical Unit or STU. He made me in charge of it and gave me an experienced detective Wayne "Slypork" Cunningham and a very clever constable Jacko Ta'ala as permanent staff. We would second extra constables or detectives as we needed them. During the following twelve months the three of us arrested about two hundred and forty people ranging from murder to traffic offences but with a strong emphasis on drugs and burglary. Jacko and Slypork made most of the arrests, as they still point out at every opportunity nowadays, stating that I was too busy telling them what to do and writing us out of trouble. All three of us also managed to finish our respective promotion exams and also take healthy lumps of leave.

It was a great year. They were two of the (many) best cops I ever worked with. We got on well despite our very different personalities and outlooks on life. Wayne was very fiery in those days and Jacko, with his calm Samoan outlook was an ideal foil for Wayne. I had no problems motivating them or controlling them and they passed on a lot of experience and knowledge to the younger members we would second on to the unit. These were sometimes constables straight from the College. They soon learned the correct way to stop and talk to criminals after watching the three of us in action.

The unit was disbanded at the end of 1987 due to pressure from the Uniform Branch for an enquiry office. This was a short sighted view of crime. There was comment made about the hours we worked, the relaxed standard of our dress and appearance, the autonomy we had within the station, and jealousy about the arrests we were making. There has always been some jealousy and conflict between CIB and Uniform Branch staff because of misconceptions about each other's role. This was apparent in this case with a Senior Sergeant demanding that the unit be disbanded so he could then have an enquiry constable at his beck and call. This particular Senior Sergeant, who is actually a great guy and a good cop, had never worked in the CIB and did not hold it in very high regard at all. It vexed him to see a Uniform Branch Sergeant and at least one Uniform Branch Constable working in the CIB office.

We were a bit upset at the time but we were also getting a bit tired. The three of us were waiting for promotion and were placed in Acting Up roles to get some experience at the higher rank before actually being promoted. I believe we made a huge dent in criminal offending in Whanganui and the small towns surrounding it. We had anecdotal evidence that crims would see the three of us and disappear because they did not want to be subject to our unique type of turn-over or street stop.

Information we received from our contacts in the underworld confirmed these stories. We were putting too much pressure on a lot of crims. Whilst the three of us were experienced cops we were really no different from a lot of our colleagues. They would, I am sure, have achieved the same results with the resources available and the freedom to use these resources, including additional staff.

I spent another period of time in the CIB before I retired. In early 1990 Peter and I swapped roles for six months on interchange. Interchange is when NCO's or Commissioned Officers swap roles to gain experience usually prior to promotion. I am not sure why Peter and I did this as neither of us was awaiting promotion to Inspector. I ran the CIB office and, overall, enjoyed my time with a great staff who did their best to keep me out of trouble. Meanwhile Pete was doing my job in Uniform making a mess of my office and not tidying up.

Dingo

Cast

Dingo –   Himself

The Farmer –   Himself

The Boxer –   Constable Paul Bass – fresh from the Royal New
                        Zealand Police College

Jacko –   Constable Jacko Ta'ala

"Gadaffi" –   Detective Wayne Cunningham a.k.a Sly or
Slypork

Rats –   Sergeant Rob Rattenbury

It was a beautiful late spring, early summer evening in the quiet suburb of Gonville, Whanganui in late 1987. Dingo, the local neighbourhood drug dealer, had just received his weekly sack of product at 7.00 p.m. for weighing and packaging for the week's work ahead. He had a busy night planned. The wife and kids were out for the evening – all was good.

What Dingo did not realise was that one of his trusted confidantes was a bit short of the readies that week so decided to talk to the local drug detective about doing a wee deal with the filth. Not an unusual process in those days.

Whilst Dingo was sitting at his dining room table he noticed a very large Pakeha male person in scruffy clothes, about 6ft 18 inches high, wearing a farmer's hat, approaching the ranch slider at the front of his house with a smaller very muscular smiling Samoan gentleman who he knew to be Jacko Ta'ala, cop and holder of at least three dans in Karate. Dingo thought that this was unusual but he then saw movement at the rear of his house. He spied two other, but especially good-looking and well-presented, gentlemen approach his back door.

One looked very angry and was saying "if you call me Gaddafi again I will punch you in the face Rats". The other, better looking one, was holding Dingo's child's tricycle for some reason and saying to his mate "Kick the door by the lock Sly not on the hinge".

Dingo was wondering momentarily what was going on when he noticed a young Police Constable in uniform running up and down the drive beside his house with a notebook in his hand. He recognized the young cop as the very well-known and renowned local boxer Paul Bass.

Dingo thought "Fuck, it's only the cops. Phew. Better get rid of the dope."

The last time this happened it was the Black Power calling and they made a real mess of the house, stealing his dope as well as making Dingo spend some quality time with the nice doctors and nurses at Good Health Whanganui. On top of that Mrs Dingo was not impressed with all the damage done to the house either. No special cuddles for Dingo for a couple of weeks.

Just as he rose from the dining room table, sack in hand he saw the giant scruffy man with a farmer's hat on kick his ranch-slider in. At the same time he saw the very good-looking chap at the back he knew as Rats throw the child's tricycle through the glass in his back door. The noise was horrendous.

Dingo's life got a bit busy about then. He threw the sack of dope over the back of the couch in the lounge, hiding it from the boys just as "His Extreme Tallness" hit him back into his dining room chair, making Dingo lose quite a bit of interest in his affairs for a while.

When Dingo was feeling a little bit better the very kind Jacko was asking him gentle questions while at the same time gently patting the back of his hand. Dingo quite liked that, at least the big farm boy was not taking any more interest in him. Dingo liked talking to the nice gentle smiling Samoan man, wanting to tell him where all the dope was and helping him get it out from behind the sofa.

Dingo saw the young boxer taking notes and the old farmer telling him not to, "waste of time Basso. He's fucked"

In the meantime the very angry good looking one Dingo knew from schooldays as a guy not to mess with was yelling at the very calm and collected, mature and refined chap who he called Rats and who seemed to be in complete command of the situation to stop laughing at him about kicking the door on the hinges.

Dingo was very happy to go with the nice gentle Jacko and the very pleasant Rats in their car back to the Police station for a cup of tea and a chat.   They then gave him a bed for the night and he rang Mrs Dingo to say that he may not be home for a wee while but could she ring Smith and Smith Glass and bring his toothbrush down to the station please.

Chapter 23

Bill and Ben the Flowerpot Men

In early 1985, a beautiful summer's weekend day in Whanganui, working an early shift with my section. Detectives Ernie Dickinson and Mark Sutherland arrive in my office to tell me that they had received some very reliable information that two well-known drug growers, Bill and Ben the flowerpot men, had just loaded their truck with freshly cut cannabis and were heading towards Whanganui from the backblocks inland from Paparangi, about 30 km north of Whanganui. Whanganui's hinterland is referred to as "tiger country". It is very rough, broken land made up of bush farms and, well, just bush. Dope growers abound in the temperate climate of the area.

Bill was from a well-known family of drug dealers and petty criminals but was known to carry firearms when undertaking drug cultivation or transit.

I grabbed Constable Wayne Mills, recently graduated from the Police College and we headed north out of town, both armed, Wayne with a .38 cal. Police revolver and me with a .223 cal. Sako Vixen Police rifle. I had arranged for AOS to be called and deployed but due to the urgency we needed to get troops in the area quickly. Ernie and Mark, also armed, headed to the other access road into the area these guys were, via Aramoho, a northern suburb of Whanganui. The plan was we would approach the area from both directions, knowing that we would come across the truck with the offenders and the dope at some stage.

Hopefully the AOS would be en route via helicopter and would arrive in time to assist.

The week before, coincidentally, I had trained my section, including Wayne, and several CIB members on how to deal with a mobile armed offender. Both Ernie and Mark were AOS-trained so I had no concerns about them, taking Wayne with me. He had impressed me at the training session so I felt he would be alright.

Wayne and I were barrelling along a dirt country road miles inland in the middle of nowhere when around the corner comes a three ton truck loaded with bales of Cannabis towards us. I had never seen so much dope in one place in my life! I threw the old Ford cop car across the narrow dirt road and we both evacuated the car, doing the standard Police drill for dealing with a suspected mobile armed offender.

The driver, Ben, got out of the truck when asked to and Wayne approached him, calling him away from the truck arrested him at gun point well away from his truck while I covered Bill who was in the passenger seat of the truck crouched down doing something. I had instructed him to remain in the truck while Wayne arrested Ben. Wayne did a great job in dealing with his first suspected armed offender. Once Ben was handcuffed and lying on the dirt road I told Bill to get out of the truck at gun point slowly and showing his hands to me at the same time. He was reluctant to do this and kept rummaging around on the floor of the truck. He eventually made the decision to get out and walked towards me, knelt on the ground when asked and I cuffed him, lying him on his belly near his mate with Wayne watching them while I searched the interior of the truck. Upon looking in the passenger foot well of the truck I found at least two dozen shot gun cartridges loose on the floor of the truck. After a cursory search I could not find any weapon.

We put Bill and Ben in the old Ford cop car, tied back to back so they could not get up to any mischief and I drove them back to Whanganui with Wayne driving the truck with all the dope.

Bill and Ben were duly charged with Possession for Supply of a Class C drug and the matter went to trial. They were making various allegations about the way Wayne and I threatened them with weapons. Bill had earlier told me he thought he had a shotgun in the truck but could not find it when we caught them thankfully as matters could have ended very differently for him. He denied saying this in Court of course but the jury found them guilty and both were sentenced to very lengthy terms of holiday care.

At some later stage we burnt all the cannabis in the station incinerator, causing all the staff, pensioners, Mums with kids and school groups in the nearby library to have a very good day!

Chapter 24 -

Some Armed Offender Squad Memories

TO CORDON, CONTAIN AND APPEAL: THE ORIGINS OF THE AOS

After being called to an incident in Bethells Rd, Waitakere, on January 6, 1963, where one Victor George Wasmuth was a roaming about with a firearm, Detective Sergeant Neville Power and Detective Inspector Wallace Chalmers were fatally shot by the gunman.

Wasmuth also shot and killed his neighbour, James Berry, and seriously wounded another man, Harry Pettit, who was visiting the area.

Police eventually apprehended Wasmuth, who was taken to Middlemore Hospital to treat an injury sustained in the stand-off. He was questioned by Detective Sergeant Bill Brien, who realised Wasmuth was mentally unbalanced. He was committed to a psychiatric institution for the rest of his life.

(Author's note - Wasmuth spent the rest of his days in the Maximum Security Unit at Lake Alice Hospital, Marton. If local Police had to visit the unit we would wear plainclothes as the sight of uniform Police used to set Wasmuth off into a rage).

In his history of the AOS, Zero-Alpha, Detective Superintendent Ray Van Beynen writes that an investigation at the time by Auckland Crown solicitor Graham Speight found fault with police planning, tactics and communication. Mr Speight made a list of suggestions on how the situation should have been handled. Some of his suggestions now form part of the AOS's Standing Operating Procedures.

Just shy of a month after the tragedy at Bethells Rd, Constables Bryan Schultz and James Richardson were called to a domestic incident in Herbert St, Lower Hutt, on February 3, 1963.

The two officers didn't even have time to switch off the engine of their car, let alone leave the car, before they were shot dead by gun-wielding Bruce McPhee kneeling at the window of his house eight metres away.

Two bystanders managed to overpower McPhee and hold him until police backup arrived. He was sentenced to life imprisonment for the double murder.

(Author's note – When young Police subsequently started duty at Lower Hutt after graduating they were always taken by the Senior Sergeant to the Police Photographer's studio and shown the photos of the scene prior to the bodies being removed and then given a lecture on how to never ever stop outside the house where a domestic is reported. This was a very sobering experience for new cops).

The deaths of four police officers in the space of four weeks shocked the country and alarmed police authorities.

Mr Brien, who had been so closely involved with the Waitakere killings, had written a report outlining the need for a specialised police squad to deal with armed offenders. As part of his research, he spent time with the New South Wales police who had an Emergency Squad that dealt with armed offenders. Mr Brien believed New Zealand Police could benefit from a similar squad. He wrote of the NSW squad: "Their primary concern is the safety of the police."

His observation was pertinent. As Mr Van Beynen notes in Zero-Alpha, the general police philosophy in New Zealand before 1963 was that it was acceptable to incur casualties with the aim of preserving an offender's life.

Mr Brien's report was submitted to Police National Headquarters on February 20, 1963, and is seen as the foundation document that helped form the AOS.

The task of setting up the squad was given to Detective Inspector Bob Walton (later commissioner), who had been closely involved with the Bethells Rd shootings, Superintendent Wattie McGuire and SAS Captain Dex Smith, who formulated policy, tactics and training.

Police were wary about the scope of the squad, believing that the public would not accept armed police, except in very limited, defensive situations. In Zero-Alpha, Mr Van Beynen notes that Walton wanted to put the onus of any action squarely on the offender, hence the name Armed Offenders Squad was chosen.

"Mr Walton believed that most situations the squad encountered could be resolved peacefully with a minimum amount of force. He said the squad's best weapon was the loud hailer or the telephone. To "cordon, contain and apeal"

was the philosophy of the squad."

He also believed in the vital role of good intelligence and the use of "appreciations and orders" (making an assessment based on all the facts available, and then carrying out a plan of action). These orders are still the basis of any AOS operation: Situation (the current situation), Mission (the aim of the operation), Execution (how this aim is going to be realised), Administration and Command and Signals (command timings and communications.)

In August 1964, the first AOS members went on a two-week training course at Papakura Military Camp. Mr Van Beynen says they were an interesting bunch – a mix of CIB and uniform from the main centres. "They were all hand-picked. You didn't apply, you were asked," he writes.

The training included a range of firearms, the use of tear gas and hand-held grenades, radio procedures and, of course, loud hailers. It wasn't long before the squad was called into action. The first recorded operation was in 1965 in the Auckland suburb of Penrose. A fifteen year old named Paul Kerry Anthony had fatally shot a sixteen year old boy and then started shooting at cars and houses in the area. The squad cordoned off the area and eventually Anthony surrendered. He was sentenced to life imprisonment.

The AOS now routinely attends nearly thousand incidents nationally each year. There are three hundred AOS members in seventeen squads around the country with six women members nationally. No AOS members have been killed during an AOS operation although AOS Sergeant Stu Guthrie was killed at Aramoana before the AOS were deployed.

All AOS members are volunteers from New Zealand Police and work on a part-time, on-call basis. All members must complete the rigorous training and selection process, the foundations of which were laid back in 1963.

The public did not initially roll out the welcome mat for the squad. New Zealand was a nation that was proud to have an unarmed police force. But, nearly fifty years on, public perception has changed and the AOS can be proud of its reputation and record for apprehending dangerous armed offenders who are a threat to public safety. -

Included Courtesy of the New Zealand Police Association Newsletter 1st December 2012, prior to the 50th Anniversary of the founding of the Police Armed Offender Squad

I was a member of the Whanganui Regional Armed Offenders Squad from 1983 to 1990, staying on as an instructor at the Police College until 1992 helping to run the AOS Qualifying Courses. I attended over 100 live operations in that time, many involving drunk offenders late at night in Whanganui and the rural areas inland to Taumaranui. Other live operations including assisting CIB undertake search warrants on gang houses and VIP protection work in the Whanganui Police district. There are many stories arising from these duties but some are too sensitive to relate here. The following chapter contains a few stories to give the reader an idea of the type of work the AOS did and still do.

Chapter 25

Some Interesting AOS Operations
Huey Dewey and Lewey

Jenny and I had moved to Whanganui in mid-1983 for a quiet life after a couple of very difficult years in Lower Hutt both personally and in terms of the Jack enquiry. We needed a rest as a family and I needed to have time to re-focus. I had started as a trainee on the local Armed Offenders Section (AOS) but, as a Sergeant, I was expected to take over as the junior Sergeant on the section in due course. The section was very ably lead by Sergeant Barry Blue, an AOS veteran of many years standing.

My first "live" operation was a cock-up from start to finish. The Whanganui section was called out on a fine summer's evening in early January 1984 to apprehend a character called Harry who information to hand indicated had travelled from the Waikato to Whanganui to kill his estranged wife. We were called out as he had been identified by the informant to be drinking in the Kai Iwi Hotel. Kai Iwi is a small settlement in Goat Valley on the road to New Plymouth about fifteen kms. north of Whanganui. I was actually called out from the Police club where Jenny and I were spending the afternoon with my sister Lynne and her then husband Peter and our kids. I had only just arrived and had started one pint of beer, a point made much of in Court and the Truth newspaper subsequently after I admitted to this in Court at one of the subsequent trials.

At the time Whanganui City station was under the supervision of a Chief Inspector. He was a good cop with years of AOS experience behind him in Wellington. He was a very strong-minded man who would brook little dissension in operational matters, preferring to lead from the front instead of leaving it to his experienced Sergeants or Senior Sergeants. A Chief Inspector's role in this type of operation was to remain at the station running the base, appointing a scene commander who, in AOS situations, is normally the AOS Sergeant or an AOS Senior Sergeant. In this case Barry Blue should have been in charge at the scene and the Chief should have remained at the station running the base.

The Chief Inspector turned up at the callout dressed in a white safari type suit. The rest of us were dressed in the AOS blue/black uniform and carrying .357 magnum pistols and .223 rifles, the normal armament for AOS at that time.

Upon leaving Whanganui station after a short briefing the Chief took Barry Blue in his car, leaving the rest of the AOS section to follow in the Team Policing van that we used in those days. A CIB car driven by a detective was ahead of us with the intention of providing early observations on the pub from a discreet distance. This was a good plan. There was no firm information that Harry was armed at the pub, but because of his stated intentions the AOS would be used to apprehend him either in the pub or on the road.

The initial plan was to form a forward base at Kai Iwi school, some five hundred metres from the hotel, and the section would then approach the hotel on foot, entering the bar simultaneously with a detective who knew Harry and taking him into custody. This was a very straightforward plan but one fraught with difficulties. What if the bar patrons turned on us? Carrying weapons hampers your ability to protect yourself from unarmed but aggressive offenders. Why not surround and hail the pub, bringing the occupants out one by one as we would normally do? There was some discussion about tactics in the van on the way and it was our intention upon arrival to discuss the tactics again with the Chief. Not an option I was personally looking forward to as, being a Sergeant, it was expected of me to point out to the Chief the problems with the proposal to rush the pub. I knew Barry would back me anyway.

Upon entering Goat Valley, about ten kms. from Whanganui, we received a radio message from the CIB car that they thought they had seen Harry heading back towards Whanganui in a white utility with two other males. A squad member in the van (Officer A) knew Harry. As the utility passed our van the member identified Harry as the driver. There had already been the CIB identification and Barry Blue also indicated that the driver looked like Harry. Upon passing us the occupants of the utility gave us the fingers. They were being closely followed by a CIB car. We turned around and gave chase.

At the Rapanui Road intersection with SH3 the utility collided with a CIB car whose driver was trying to stop it. We were concerned about chasing the utility back into town bearing in mind the time of day, about 5.30 p.m., and the number of innocent people about.

The ute was followed down Francis Road, right into Mosston Road and left into Buxton Road where it was stopped by the Chief running it off the road with his unmarked car. A general melee ensued with Police removing the occupants quickly from the ute. In the van we were concerned about getting to the ute as fast as possible, bearing in mind we had an identification on the suspect who had clearly shown by his actions that he was not going to stop for the Police. An AOS cop and I grabbed the front seat passenger by the door, falling into a deep roadside ditch with him, closely followed by another AOS cop and the middle seated occupant. We subdued and handcuffed these two suspects. The driver was removed by other squad members together with the Chief.

What should have happened is we should have followed the van until it stopped and called on the occupants from a safe distance to vacate the vehicle one at a time to be taken into custody separately and away from the utility vehicle. That plan went out the window with the Chief running the truck off the road.

At about this stage several assaults took place on the driver, the later enquiry establishing that the offenders being the Chief, Officer A, who initially identified Harry to us in the van and one other AOS member (Officer B). One of the allegations faced by the Chief was that he tortured the driver, a petty criminal named Huey, by pulling his chest hairs out to get him to admit who he was. The Chief was beside himself because of the damage done to at least one Police vehicle during the chase. We soon established that none of the occupants were Harry. They were three likely lads, Huey, Dewey and Luey, not altogether choir boys, but certainly not guilty of any major offences.

At that point the Police, namely the Chief, should have backed off. We took the three to Whanganui station and Barry, another sergeant Terry Gray and I discussed the incident and any offences involved with the Chief. He was in a highly agitated emotional state. His shirt had been ripped in the struggle with Huey and his beloved Police cars had taking a bit of a hiding. He was not in the mood to discuss the criminal charges, if any, which could be bought against the three. They were to be charged and that was that.

We urged him to release the three into the care of their lawyer John Rowan QC. We could then look at the evidence available to support or not support charges. I was particularly careful to take full written notes due to the Jack incident two years previously. I was not going down that path again. I asked the Chief to reconsider the decision to hold the three men. He was adamant that they would stay in the cells. He bought a fight with John Rowan and the Police Department with that decision. It would result in his eventual dismissal from the Police, being convicted of assault after a long and highly honourable career.

John Rowan duly lodged a complaint with the Police about the incident and the way his clients had been treated. I thought "not again". This time I was convinced we had made a serious misjudgement in holding the three men. I still believe that if they had been released the Chief would have kept his job. The mood he was in that day, if we had released Huey, Dewey and Luey I believe the Chief would have tried to lock us up!

After previous dealings I had had with the Chief in Wellington prior to coming to Whanganui I considered that he was slightly unbalanced at times. He was a very popular commander with his staff and with the Police hierarchy but he was prone to quite emotional behaviour. He had previous incidents where he had dealt with staff in a very unsatisfactory manner. If you had any ambition or just wanted a quiet life you did not upset him.

Traffic charges were laid against the three men. These were duly dismissed after a protracted Court hearing. The Police enquiry rolled on for some months with most of the squad, myself included, subject to close scrutiny about the way we handled the incident. I was counselled for sticking my pistol down the throat of the male I removed from the utility. It seemed a good idea at the time as he was, in my mind at the time, an armed suspect. As we had to rush the utility because of where the Chief was parked, to ensure his and Barry's safety, we were forced to be quite heavy with the occupants.

The Chief and one AOS member (Officer B) faced assault charges. Officer A did not face any charges after making a deal with the department to implicate the Chief and his AOS squad mate. None of the rest of us was in a position to see what the Chief and Officer A had done as we all had our hands full. The Chief was easily identified by nearby members of the public as he was dressed in white, when the rest of us were in black and he was the only one at the scene going off his scone.

After another long trial both officers were convicted of assault. Officer A kept his job, a very unusual decision at that time, but was removed from the AOS. The Chief was dismissed from the Police for his actions both at the scene and later in the station. Both also received fines. Officer B who did the deal left the squad within a short while for "psychological reasons". A move welcomed by the rest of us as we could no longer trust him in a tight situation.

What happened to Harry? A day or so after the chase we got information that he was holed up in a farm house at Maxwell, north of Whanganui. We mounted a normal AOS operation surrounding the house at dawn, hailing the house, with Harry coming out to give himself up. He was arrested without incident. The Whanganui AOS was then non-operational for some months because of the enquiry. I thought that this was a great start to my

AOS career, first live operation and I am in the shit again.

Tigertooth

In 1985 the Wanganui AOS was called to a hostage taking operation in suburban Palmerston North. We were called out at about 5.00 p.m. arriving at the scene at about 6.30 p.m. Walking from the Safe Arrival Point we could hear shots being fired from what sounded like a heavy calibre rifle. We moved into position around a house on a back section, boosting the Palmerston North AOS who were already in position.

The offender was inside a wooden house and had a female hostage. He was talking by phone to a local radio station and also to hostage negotiators at the local Police station. He was quite irrational and referred to himself as simply "Tigertooth". Periodically he would fire shots at random through the walls of the house. He fired at several of us as we moved into cover. It is amazing how small you can become when a heavy calibre rifle is being fired at you. We could not respond as we could not see the offender. We also did not know where the hostage was. We remained in position all night, once we were in position it was dangerous to try and leave. Just on dawn we were relieved by the Wellington and New Plymouth AOS.

All this time the offender was talking to the HNT. We never saw the offender or the hostage. He allowed the hostage to go later in the morning of the following day and gave himself up shortly afterwards. I never got to meet the guy who had tried to kill several of us. He was well known to the Palmerston North Police and had, some months earlier, fired on Police on State Highway 1 near Himatangi when they were trying to arrest him for stealing a farmer's truck. He was regarded as a very dangerous dude.

To give some idea of his mental state, when he was arrested for the earlier incident he was wearing twin holsters and in one holster he had a Pinky chocolate bar. He got a lengthy term of imprisonment of kidnapping and assorted other crimes, there being no evidence to support attempted murder charges other than holes on the house walls and changes of underwear for most of us.

This was a successful operation as no one got hurt or shot.

Smith – Not real name

Smith and his family lived with extended whanau on land north of Taumarunui towards Ongarue. In 1985 the local Police were called by hospital staff to hear that the body of a three year old female child had been dropped at the hospital by Smith and his wife. Initial examination showed that the child had suffered severe head injuries prior to death.

Smith was suspected by the local Police to be in possession of firearms and had a reputation for violence. He was regarded as very anti-Police. He was a patched Mongrel Mob member who would not willingly accompany the Police anywhere.

He was also related to Daniel Houpapa, a gang member shot dead by Police in Taumarunui after an armed stand-off in 1976. Due to this incident there is a very strong anti-Police attitude in parts of the Taumarunui community associated with the Mongrel Mob gang.

Because of these reasons it was decided by the Senior Sergeant at Taumarunui that the AOS would be used to approach and take Smith into custody. Both the Whanganui and Palmerston North AOS sections were called to Taumarunui, with New Plymouth mobilised as well, but as reserve due to the distance involved.

Barry Blue and I approached the collection of run down houses where Smith lived in complete darkness at about 1.30 a.m. to undertake a reconnoitre of the terrain. We managed to move the Whanganui Section into a cordon around the cabin we had identified as likely to contain Smith and his wife. We then awaited the Palmerston North section. It would be easier to contain the area, which is in semi-bush, amongst hills, with both sections before calling on Smith to come out.

We duly called on Smith to come out after the Palmy boys arrived but we got no response after about an hour of calling. At this I crawled to the back of the hut, cutting a hole in the plastic window, and surveyed the darkened building. It was obvious that there were people present, the warmth and smell telling me this.

By this time we had found out from relations that Smith had no firearms and the decision was made to rush the cabin. The idea was to put two Police dogs into the building to soften Smith up. I cannot recall why we did not use gas, but it may be because of the inflammable qualities of the building's materials. Tear gas grenades actually emit strong flames when releasing the gas, usually resulting in a fire.

The two dogs went in and there were loud shouts, thumps, dogs barking and growling. Not much else happened so a few of us, including the two handlers, rushed into the hut. The dogs were hanging on to Smith, but he did not appear fazed by this. About four of us threw ourselves at Smith, knocking him onto his back and getting bitten on the legs by the two dogs for our troubles. Smith had no intention of coming peacefully and it took the strength of all four of us plus the two dogs to hold him down, let alone handcuff him. He was a very big, strong man and used to fighting.

We managed to get Smith under control and he was eventually interviewed and charged with the murder of his daughter. The little girl received her injuries when Smith back handed her at the dinner table for not eating her tea. She died of severe head injuries.

Smith's home was a hut with no power and a dirt floor. He lived in this abode with his wife and children. Other homes nearby were of similar make. Amazing in late 20th century New Zealand.

Bell Block – New Plymouth

This will show how bad things can go and how quick they change in a frightful situation.

In 1987 I was the Sergeant in charge of the Whanganui section of the Armed Offenders Squad. Whanganui and Palmerston North AOS were called to Bell Block outside New Plymouth to assist the New Plymouth AOS in what was a home invasion kidnapping and hostage taking incident.

The two offenders were brothers from Bell Block. During the early hours of the morning they were seen interfering with cars in a quiet cul-de-sac in suburban Bell Block. Upon being disturbed one of them fired a shot at the public witness and they both forced their way into a flat occupied by a young couple. The night shift cops from New Plymouth were called by neighbours hearing shouts and screams in their street. Upon arriving at the scene the cops were faced with a hostage situation with the brothers threatening to kill the young couple. They had barricaded themselves inside the couple's flat and, we would discover later, booby-trapped the door-handles with electric wiring connected to the mains electricity.

This was beyond the scope of the duty shift section to deal with so the New Plymouth AOS were eventually summonsed. Upon arrival they confirmed that they had a hostage situation and that it was not going to be a straight-forward operation to rescue the two young people and capture the two brothers. Because of the seriousness of the incident they called out the Whanganui and Palmerston North sections together with the Hostage Negotiation Team from Palmerston North.

At the time Whanganui had just received a brand new Ford truck set up as a mobile communications base for taking to a safe point near any AOS operation. This would be where the Scene Commander, usually an Inspector of Senior Sergeant, and radio operator would base themselves. The Commander could then co-ordinate the operation and was able to access more assistance if needed. It even had a very early mobile phone which looked like a brick with an aerial.

When these vans were designed no real thought was given to the distances that some squads have to travel. The fuel capacity of our brand new van was so limited we could not travel to New Plymouth from Whanganui (about 160 km) on one tank of gas. On this particular call out we had to stop at Eltham to re-fuel. The van was heavily laden with radio equipment, our lights and other tactical gear so was always probably over-loaded.

Upon our arrival at the scene the Whanganui AOS was placed into cordons on the front and left side of the couple's property and negotiations commenced with the guys. It soon became apparent that they were heavily intoxicated or drugged. They would not listen to reason for some time but, after about two hours, let the two hostages go. They then left the address armed with the rifle, a softball bat and a sword. The guy with the sword made straight for my position in the cordon with his brother closely following. It was clear that they were going to attack myself and another AOS member. This then became the classic "Shoot, Don't Shoot" scenario for me. I could not get away as I was backed into a tree. My mate managed to pull back a bit. I pointed my revolver at the guy armed with the sword and told him he was under arrest and to put the weapon down or I would shoot him. He continued to approach and I repeated my request. He was by now about five metres from me and approaching at a slow deliberate walk. I committed myself to the shooting when a hostage negotiator walked behind the subject. I was using a .357 magnum and at that range the bullet would have gone through the subject and struck the cop behind. I had no choice but to stand there. An AOS member from New Plymouth called out suddenly to the subject by name and he averted his head, momentarily distracted from me. I then left my position.

Both subjects were then attacked by Police dogs with little effect, one dog nearly being killed by the softball bat. As we only had firearms, no pepper spray or tasers in those days, we could not get near the offenders who were using their weapons to keep us away. Apart from the incident I described, we were not justified in shooting them.

The two brothers really wanted to make a fight of it and had no intention of giving themselves up without a struggle.

We decided to rush them and an AOS member picked up a ten foot drainage pipe and managed to floor one of the offenders with this. At this we all managed to get inside the weapons and arrest the two offenders after a very violent struggle. They were both sentenced to lengthy terms of imprisonment. A very nasty incident.

At the time, and subsequently, we faced some criticism from one Police member present (not a squad member) for not shooting the offender approaching me. I remember being very upset at this. If I had shot him I would also have killed the Hostage Negotiator who managed somehow to get himself in the wrong place at exactly the wrong time. He actually saved the offender's life. It is bad enough having to deal with shooting a person without also having to cope with accidentally killing another cop in the process.

Chapter 26

More War Stories

Armed Offender Squad Qualifying Course

In about 1989 the Police decided to put in place a course designed for Police interested in working on the Armed Offender Squads around the country. This would be based at the Royal New Zealand Police College and run by the National Firearms and Tactics Co-ordinator, Chief Inspector Taffy Jones and his side-kick Inspector Murray Forbes. The actual instructors would come from the Sergeants and Senior Sergeants, both uniform Branch and Criminal Investigation Branch members of the Armed Offender Squads (AOS) around New Zealand. I was volunteered due to my role as Officer in Charge of the Whanganui AOS and then Second in Charge of the Whanganui-Manawatu-Taranaki Regional Armed Offenders Squad. The college would supply the Firearms Instructors.

We ran the first two week course in early 1989, my fellow instructors being Senior Sergeant Ray Sutton from Rotorua, Sergeant Jimmy McLaughlin from Wellington and Sergeant Graeme Wilkes from Nelson. Our job was to teach aspiring AOS members of all ranks, including Commissioned Officers, the fundamental philosophy of the Armed Offenders Squad which is cordon, contain and appeal, with variations as the need arises. We also taught the relevant law around use of deadly force, namely shooting people. The students also learned tactics, foot patrol-work, moving across rough country or in urban areas without being seen, communications procedures, map-reading, writing orders groups and plans - all good boy-scout stuff. They also had to undertake a twenty four hour bush exercise with a mobile armed offender to deal with in an isolated bush area near Wellington, staying out all night in the bush. Very real.

During the course the students were also assessed on their abilities to fit into a team situation and also underwent psychological assessment for obvious reasons.

Whilst course members were of different ranks, while they were on the course they were all regarded as trainees and were required to take part in all aspects of the course, including the reasonably high standard of physical training. This normally went well but we did have one Inspector on the course who just could not get his head around this aspect.

He came to the course after being nominated by his District as no other Commissioned Officer in the District wanted to be on the Squad.

When he became stressed he would get quite vocal and upset. Not good qualities for an AOS Commander. We were on a twenty four hour bush exercise in the foot hills of the Tararua Ranges behind Otaki when he approached me and said he wanted to make a complaint of assault against one of the other course members. We had all been up for at least twenty four hours without sleep so I guess some irritable behaviour is understandable. I asked him what happened and he told me that he was climbing a bank when the cop in front of him slipped and stood on his head by mistake. I asked him why he wanted to make a complaint. He replied that the cop laughed at him when he remonstrated with him for his clumsiness. I asked the

Inspector to think about this for a while and perhaps sleep on it. He then got a bit shouty at me. I walked off, ignoring him and leaving Taffy Jones to sort him out.

Upon arrival back to the College he was still going on. Nothing was done of course. For this and other reasons this member should not have passed the course but the District needed an Inspector to run their local Armed Offender Squad so he was passed. It made a bit of a joke of the course really when we had young cops working their butts off to get onto the squad, some being failed and having to come back again to re-sit. Not a good morale-booster when they see the odd Wally get pushed through.

If the students passed, usually on the recommendations of the instructors and the psychologists, they would return to their home districts to await a vacancy on their home squads.

On later courses we were also joined by Detective Sergeant Pat Coghlan from Whangarei and Detective Sergeant Derek Webb from Taumaranui, a very experienced and knowledgeable AOS member from the Auckland district.

We tended to pass most students which is a testimony to how well the districts handled the original applications. Sometimes a student was passed for reasons other than competence, such as a Commissioned Officer being passed as there was no one in his district who would take on the Squad duties. Nothing to do with us minions.

I helped to run three courses at the College and really enjoyed my time there.

Motorcade Squad

In 1990 Auckland was to host the Commonwealth Games. The Queen and the Duke of Edinburgh would be staying in Auckland during the games, together with other members of the Royal Family. As part of the massive security operation for the games the Police decided to supplement the existing Anti-Terrorist Squad with selected staff from Armed Offender Squads in New Zealand. In 1989 twenty-five staff were selected on the basis of experience and availability. Lance Tebbutt and I were selected from Whanganui and we spent all of 1989 in various parts of New Zealand, usually on military bases, being trained in the use of automatic weapons, tactics, house clearing, and driving offensively as part of a motorcade. Great time was had by all. This was all Boy's Own Stuff.

We had a fleet of old Police cars, rental cars and even stock cars to use. We normally worked with driving instructors from the Diplomatic Protection Squad or with SAS and other military personnel. Our main instructors were experienced Anti-Terrorist Squad members. Our job was to form part of the Royal Motorcade and to shadow the motorcade in case of terrorist attack. We managed to wreck most of the cars during the training.

Operationally we used plain Police vehicles and wore plainclothes. We were armed with Heckler and Koch MP5 sub machine guns as primary weapons carried in loose carry bags and our personal .357 Smith & Wesson Magnum pistols in shoulder holsters. We also had access to other weaponry as required. Our role was to shadow any Royal Motorcade and reinforce ATS staff involved in any armed incident or attack on the Royal Party. During the operation we were accommodated at a hotel opposite Cornwall Park in Epsom.

The operation went off without a hitch. We had a great boss, Mike Crawford, who looked after us and ran a tight ship.

By this time I was a Senior Sergeant and, as I was no longer as active operationally on AOS as I had been I was looking at calling it quits on AOS to concentrate on other portfolios I was responsible for such as prosecutions, staff training and gang liaison. I was also required to undertake internal enquiries for the then Police Complaints Authority which, by their very nature, are very time consuming and intense.

The two weeks at the Games was my last AOS operation, I resigned from the Squad upon my return to Wanganui in February 1990. I still stayed informally involved with the squad both locally and as an instructor on the AOS Qualifying Course at the Police College in Porirua. My colleague Neville Haggart took the squad over in early 1990.

The Famous Five have fun in Foxton

Working as a member of the New Zealand Police Armed Offenders Squad was always a deadly serious job. But at times things would not go quite as planned. The following little tale shows what can happen when fate conspires against good management and bad luck intervenes. Luckily no animals were seriously hurt in the unfolding of these events.

Early one fine summer day in about 1985 five good chums, members of the Whanganui Armed Offenders Squad, left town to attend a combined training exercise with another AOS group in the forested sandhill area near Foxton, a small country town on the coast south of Whanganui. They stopped at Sanson to buy sausage sandwiches and fruit juice for lunch. Thus catered for they sallied forth down the famous Foxton Straights (the road not the trousers) in their old CF Bedford prison van to meet the other members of the exercise.

The five chums spent the day playing in the sandhills near Foxton, pretending to shoot and tear-gas people and take prisoners and otherwise have a really jolly time with all their other pals in black. They were enjoying themselves so much that they forgot to have lunch.

As the day drew to a close it was decided by popular vote for all the chaps involved in the day's activities to adjourn to a nearby hostelry for light refreshments and to discuss all the good fun that they had had during the day. The Whanganui chums ate their sausage sandwiches because by then they were very very hungry. Before going into the local tavern they had locked all their guns and things that go bang away in the old CF Bedford van.

Over the next hour or so great tales of derring-do were told and much hilarity ensued. The chums had nominated one of their number as the sober driver. He also kept a weather eye on the vehicles in the car park.

In the little village of Foxton at the time lived an ogre and he had a lot of ogre friends. They wore leathers and patches and liked to scare nice people. They did not like the chums and their friends and did not like them being in the little village. The ogre got one of his very junior ogres to walk around all the nice police vehicles in the dark and cut the tyres. The sober drivers did not notice anything amiss. The ogre then came into the hostelry to engage in friendly banter with the chums and their friends. The chums and their friends decided that they would have to now go home as they were getting tired and it was dark and the ogre and his friends were being very mean to them. The chums then noticed that they had a flat tyre as others also did. The ogre and his pals then playfully teased the chums and it all got very physical, as it sometimes does with boys.

The ogre and his mates all decided that they did not want to play anymore as the chums and their pals got very mean and nasty when they found what the ogres had done to their vehicles.

The five chums from Whanganui fixed their flat tyre and got into their old CF Bedford van and began motoring home back up the Foxton Straights. On the way they heard over the radio that the ogres had gone to the local Police station in Foxton and fire-bombed it. The five chums from Whanganui all wondered what to do. The oldest and wisest chum said "keep driving" so they did.

Chapter 27

Something a bit lighter

Not all Police work has to be about crime, drama and tragedy –
The following two stories are about community events I was
proud to be involved in while a Police Officer.

Helping the Community

Back in the late seventies and eighties jogging was the thing to
do. I was into it, as were all my work mates and friends. People
were running half marathons, marathons, fun runs, ten km runs
and sponsored runs.

Looking back it seems we were all a lot slimmer then. As a cop
running was an excellent way to keep fit for chasing our clients
so many cops spent a lot of time putting the miles in.

One very enterprising colleague of mine, Laurie Gabites, thought
running would be a good idea to make some money for his
favourite charity, the Te Omanga Hospice in Lower Hutt. With
the support of the Police administration and the help of another
colleague, Noel Wynne, Laurie organized the first run to raise
money for the hospice in late 1979. This was very successful so
Laurie decided to make it an annual event.

In 1980 I found myself back at Lower Hutt and being a mad
jogger (never a runner) got roped into the deal. Having had
cancer some years before I was very supportive of the hospice

ethos and jumped onto the band wagon with a lot of very fit and motivated work mates.

In November 1980 twenty five of us together with radio announcer Brian Waddell set off for Rotorua with the intention of running back to Lower Hutt, raising money via sponsorship and street collections for the hospice. We were away for a week and ran a relay between Rotorua and Lower Hutt via New Plymouth, raising about $4,500 for the hospice. All staff took annual leave for this event and the Police provided a couple of vehicles, with Brian accompanying us every year. Guthrie Coach Lines provided a tourist coach which we pretty much lived in for the week and a very patient driver Alan, who put up with us. Cobb & Co and the Air Force provided accommodation and meals with some re-hydration product as well.

The running was the easy part. We were all very fit and each ran three km legs two to four times per day each, eating up the distance. At each town, if one was not running one was out collecting, this was the work part of the deal.

I did three runs, stopping when I left Lower Hutt to transfer to Whanganui in 1983. I loved it. The last run I was involved in raised over $42,000 for the hospice, clearing its mortgage. A lot of money back in 1982. We ran from Auckland one year and then from Gisborne another year. By this time Laurie had involved the Fire Service as well and they ran a run at the same time but on a different course.

In those days Mardi Gras was a big thing in Lower Hutt and we always timed our run to arrive at about 7.00 p.m. on the evening of the annual Mardi Gras. This was a big deal, something we do not see much of nowadays unfortunately. The whole city stopped and the main street was awash with entertainment and stalls. The Police pipe band would bring us in. The run had been on 2ZB all week so the buildup was intense to say the least. The mayor would welcome us and Laurie would hand the annual cheque to the hospice there and then. A big deal. It made me very proud to be involved.

Well done Laurie, your idea, drive and motivation made a huge difference to a lot of families.

Ratana

For two or three years in the mid to late eighties I had the privilege of leading the Police contingent at the annual Ratana celebrations near Whanganui. Every year in late January thousands of adherents of the Ratana faith gather at the Ratana village to celebrate the birthday of the prophet T W Ratana on January 25th. Leaders of all political parties also attend to strut their stuff to the followers hoping to garner the Maori vote, especially in election year.

Followers come from all over New Zealand and Australia as well as the wider world. The celebrations normally run for the week up to the prophet's birthday. People gather to attend religious events, play sport, take part in cultural activities and catch up with whanau and friends. It is a very peaceful place with a festival atmosphere normally. One year we had approximately 25,000 attendees.

Because of the numbers of people involved and one or two incidents at the village during the celebrations in previous years the Church Morehu (Servants) asked the Police for some support. Whanganui Police would usually send a Sergeant, the Country

Enquiry constable and several other Constables, including Community and Maori Constables to the celebrations for the week. I always liked to include at least one Pakeha Constable who would be working outside his or her comfort zone in a total Maori environment as a learning experience for them.

The Police would work in support of and with the Church wardens or Katipa. The Church Wardens (Kaitiaki-Whakamoemiti) are responsible for keeping peace and order in the Worship Service and recording attendance during the Worship Service (Whakamoemiti).

They wear uniform and on the marae their word is the law as representatives of the President and the Morehu. They were all physically very big and/or physically able men and women held in great respect by the Church. Of course people are also subject to NZ law as well, hence the attendance of Police.

We would base ourselves in the Wardens office in the Manawa, the church buildings, and provide support with telecommunications and transport as necessary. Police would work one on one with the wardens on the marae but let the wardens lead the way in all matters.

One such matter was a road block at the only road access to the marae where the wardens would search every vehicle coming into the village and confiscate all alcohol. We took very much a back seat at this checkpoint unless we were asked for assistance or there was a breach of criminal law. We also were able to keep a close eye on who was attending, including gang members from around the country. They were not permitted to be patched on the marae but were identifiable in other ways to us. If we wanted to turn them over we would wait until they left the village and stop them on the public roads, taking details for intelligence purposes. Any arrests during the week usually came from this.

In those days the Black Power gang from Wellington attended every year to work the rubbish trucks for the Church. They otherwise maintained a very low, law-abiding profile while on the marae. It was other gangs that caused problems at times.

One year a gang from Tauranga waited until they saw the on duty Police leave the marae late in the evening and then waited until the Wardens were busy. They then stabbed a member of another gang on the marae in front of the pae pae during a function. We had been called away to an incident in one of the pubs nearby. With the assistance of the wardens and the community we identified the offenders and arrested them. The gang was thrown off the marae by the Wardens at the request of the President of the Church.

In those days there were three pubs close to the marae so these usually did a roaring trade during the week as no alcohol was allowed in the village. This sometimes led to issues with fights and drink-driving which we dealt with as and when needed. Being country pubs though most trouble was well sorted before we arrived.

We worked long shifts, usually starting late morning and not finishing until after the pubs closed each night. Any arrests were taken back to Whanganui for processing. We usually did foot patrols in the village, engaging with people and, at times, taking part in the festival activities and doing mobile patrols with a Warden around the perimeter area and roads to stop alcohol being smuggled into the village.

Relations between the Police and the Church were, in my time, excellent. At the end of the celebrations we often had Constables who enjoyed their duty on the marae so much that they continued to visit people they had met and who had befriended them. These were usually the ones I thought would be out of their comfort zones. The benefit arising from this is that we then had Constables who could see the world through a slightly different lens, achieving an understanding of a different culture and making them more rounded as people in a very bicultural district such as Whanganui.

Chapter 28

Senior Sergeant

Getting a bit serious now

1988 beckoned and so did promotion to Senior Sergeant.
When I first joined the Police I was asked by my Police instructor what level or rank I would aspire to and I said then that Senior Sergeant was the level I would want to reach. I never really considered becoming an Inspector despite sitting the required exams and university papers. Commissioned rank was too distant from the actual role of policing that I joined for. I did the exams anyway - never know what the future holds.

However in those days promotion to Inspector would have meant a transfer to Wellington or Auckland to work around the clock on section shifts again. The dreaded five week roster. Not a very attractive proposition to put to the family when asking them to change their lives again. Jen had a good job and the ankle-biters were in good schools.

In early 1988 a vacancy occurred at Whanganui for a Uniform Branch Senior Sergeant. One of the requirements for the role was that the applicant had Armed Offender Squad experience as either a Sergeant or Senior Sergeant as the successful applicant would need to be second-in-charge of the Whanganui Regional Armed Offender Squad, a group of up to forty staff, including up to ten dog handlers based in Palmerston north, Whanganui and New Plymouth. The term "second in charge" is a Police term for the guy or girl who actually does all the organizing, planning and staff selection on any group or squad. The Officer in charge, usually an Inspector or Detective Inspector, offers oversight, support, mentoring and command experience but the poor old 2 I/C is the worker.

The vacancy was written just for a chappie like me. I had finished my promotion exams for the rank of Senior Sergeant the previous year and had been in an Acting role for some months actually doing the job but receiving a higher duties allowance. By 1988 I had been on the Armed Offender Squad for five years and had been the Sergeant in Charge of the AOS section based in the Whanganui station with ten staff, for about three years so had the necessary qualifications for the command role on the Regional Squad.

I duly applied for the role, receiving strong support and recommendation from my Area Commander Chief Inspector John Palmer or "JP". As far as I can recall there were only two applicants for the role, probably due to the specialisation involved, myself and Detective Sergeant Earl Mason. Earl was based in the Whanganui CIB office and had been stationed at Whanganui since joining the Police. He had not served on the AOS in his career. We got on well and I respected his abilities as a detective.

Within a week or two of applying I was informed I had been recommended for promotion to Senior Sergeant at Whanganui (Second in charge Regional AOS Squad). Brilliant. In those days applicants were not normally interviewed for roles unless there was doubt about selection. The "Best person for the Role" test was applied based on the applicant's job experience, fit for the new role, seniority and the comments from supervisors.

Back then once it was publicly announced that a person had been recommended by the Promotion Board for selection there was a fourteen day period for any other applicant for the role to lodge an Appeal against the recommendation of the Promotion Board.

Everybody congratulated me on the recommendation. Earl was somewhat quiet about matters. He is a quiet chap anyway so I did not think anything of it.

On the last day of the Appeal period JP called me into his office after 4.00 p.m. to tell me that Earl had waited until the last minute but had applied for an Appeal against my promotion. I was stunned to say the least. I was actually doing the job anyway but as a Sergeant. Earl had never served on the AOS. He had very limited operational experience as a Detective in a provincial station and on paper did not stack up against me at all in terms of experience at running a Uniform Branch section or actually running a large station and district as an Acting Senior Sergeant. Earl was a good investigator but I had also worked as an investigator for some years in Wellington and Whanganui, having worked on more homicides and other serious crime than him. Lastly, in those days seniority in rank still mattered to some extent and I was senior to Earl as a Sergeant. Earl is a very intelligent guy so I could not work out what he was doing. We could not now, obviously, talk to each other until the Appeal had been disposed of one way or the other. We maintained our distance but in a small station this can be difficult.

This now meant that I had to personally convince the Promotions Board that I was the "best person for the role". This would mean a hearing in front of the Board with both Earl and I and our respective representatives outlining our cases for why we each should have the job. Not a pleasant experience when I thought

Earl was a mate.

Over the next few months I beavered away preparing my case whilst still working as an Acting Senior Sergeant in the job that I had been recommended to be promoted for. Things were a bit tense at times but we both carried on as before. Any gloss about being promoted had long worn off by now. Everyone commiserated with me and seemed to be on my side and Earl seemed to become quite disaffected. If Earl had won the Appeal I could have worked for him as my Senior Sergeant both in the station and on AOS but he seemed to have an issue with me becoming a Senior Sergeant for some reason.

Prior to the Appeal Hearing both parties were required to serve on the other the evidence that they would be relying on to support their applications. Earl and I did this. Reading Earl's submission I felt a lot better as there was nothing in the submission that I could not answer well and rebut as the "Best person for the role".

A few days before the Appeal Hearing I was again summonsed to JP's office to be informed that Earl had abandoned his appeal application and that my promotion had been confirmed. JP then laughingly ordered me to get my stripes off and get the Senior Sergeant crown sewn on my sleeve before they change their minds.

Again I got congratulated by my peers and staff and was, at last, able to quietly celebrate my promotion with Jenny and the kids.

I decided to give Earl a few days before I approached him. When I did talk to Earl he was not a happy camper. Any friendship I thought we had was no longer evident. I felt sorry about this but if Earl was not big enough to move on then it probably showed why he may not get further promotion. It is all about leadership and a forgiving and understanding nature contributes towards the qualities of good leadership.

Earl took time off work not long after this and a few weeks later I was out on my daily jog (shuffle) around the bridges of Whanganui when I saw two of my colleagues, Mark Chillingworth and Neville Haggart, running towards me. These guys are runners, not shufflers like me. As they passed me they yelled out that Earl had applied to "Perf" or take early retirement from the Police. I looked at them, unable to talk due to trying to breathe, and waved weakly. They laughed and motored off at sub five minute mile pace. I felt really sorry for Earl. He was a family man with two school-age children but he had been having some difficulties recently, I think the Appeal issue not helping. I never saw Earl again until after I, myself "perfed" four years later. By then Earl was established in the Insurance industry and was very successful. He was also very happy. I let him sell me a superannuation scheme which over the years proved very very profitable. He now lives in Australia and is, by all accounts, a very successful businessman. I wish him only well as he is a good guy.

A duty Senior Sergeant's position in a provincial station looked alright to me and it was. I was still active on the AOS but with promotion was required to take a step backwards to administration with the need to run the odd live operation. I handed the actual running of the section over to Mark Chillingworth, a very able uniform sergeant. One good thing was not quite as many callouts in the middle of the night. He was ably assisted by Bob Burns as his second in charge.

I now had the Squad Senior Sergeant's job with Chief Inspector John Palmer as the Regional Head of the AOS. The actual squad included the AOS sections from New Plymouth, Palmerston North and Whanganui with Whanganui as the HQ station. The squad at any one time had a commissioned officer in charge with a Senior Sergeant as second in charge, at least six Sergeants or Detective Sergeants and about twenty Constables or Detectives. We also had about ten dog handlers on attachment to the squad. Quite a large body of people to administer, train and supervise. We also worked with a Hostage Negotiation Team based in Palmerston North.

Over the seven years I was involved in the Whanganui AOS I probably attended about one hundred live operations, maybe more, maybe less. Most were basic cordon, contain, appeal & arrest of usually drunk or angry men in the early hours of the morning. But others were memorable as you would have seen from previous stories.

Later in 1988, some months after I was promoted to Senior Sergeant, I was advised by JP that I had to attend a Senior Sergeant Qualifying course at the Royal New Zealand Police College in Porirua. I asked JP if I could be excused as I knew I was to be away from home for most of 1989 on AOS and Anti-Terrorist Squad training for the upcoming Commonwealth Games and Royal Tour in early 1990. I was also to be an instructor at the College for about a month on the first AOS Qualifying Course to be run in New Zealand.

From memory the Senior Sergeant Qualifying Course was only two weeks long but I was already a Senior Sergeant so I did not feel that I should have to attend a "qualifying course". I tried to explain this to the boss but he would have none of it, saying that

I would enjoy the experience. I had a couple of projects on the go and was working on an internal investigation following a complaint made about the alleged actions or inactions of Police that needed finalising for the sake of the parties involved, the complainants and the cops I had been investigating. JP blithely waved those away, wishing me well at the course.

I must admit I did not bring my best attitude to this course. When I got there I found there were only a few substantive Senior Sergeants like me and the rest of the course was Sergeants qualified by exam for promotion. This was the beginning of the way promotions were to be done in the Police in future, probably for the better. I was just unlucky to be between the old style management course that had been offered up to then for substantive Senior Sergeants and the new style "qualifying" course for Sergeants qualified by exam.

The Course Co-ordinator and I knew each other from Wellington days and we were not good friends, him spending most of his time in training while mugs like me went out in the rain to do actual Police work. I contributed to class discussions and offered my advice on planning sessions, something I was very experienced at from running AOS operations and felt that my advice was welcome. Others on the course had, overall, good, strong and interesting backgrounds in Policing so it was an interesting course to attend in a lot of ways.

I did, sometimes, turn up late for class due to going to the gym at lunchtime, visiting friends or family after class and staying overnight, getting back to the college late, and generally deciding that the particular subject of the lesson I was late for was not of great importance to me. I did not have to qualify for anything so did not feel the urge to try very hard.

At the end of the course I had to meet with the Course Co-ordinator for my assessment. He did not pull any punches saying that my contribution was minimal at best, my attitude towards the course was abysmal, that I was rude to visiting speakers on occasions. I had to agree. Some of the visitors were openly anti-Police and I did not see why I should sit quiet while they belittled a job and people I am very proud of. I then asked if I could go as I had a bus to catch back to Whanganui where I actually had some real and pressing Police work awaiting for my early attention. I also told him that there was nothing he could do about my assessment anyway as I was already a Senior Sergeant and was not intending to go further up the greasy pole (take further promotion).

Upon arriving back to work a day or two later I was asked by JP how the course went. I told him it was a waste of my time and that he would be getting quite a bad report about me.

When the report arrived he was shocked to say the least. I told him that the prick running the course was not a friend of mine and had never been one so I was never going to get a good report. I told JP that this was evident from about day one so I just decided to enjoy myself, contribute where I could but otherwise sit back and let matters take their course.

Poor old JP did not know what to do. I told him not to worry too much as I wasn't. I then moved on to more real matters awaiting me.

Apart from the AOS duties I was also responsible for prosecutions, training of Police in the Whanganui district, running a suburban Community Policing Centre, conducting internal enquiries on behalf of the new Police Complaints

Authority and normal operational day-to-day policing on shifts with callouts in Whanganui. I also carried on as a relief prosecutor and did some gang liaison work. Full days.

Police Complaints Authority (Now called the Independent Police Complaints Authority)

Prior to 1989, complaints against the Police were investigated internally by Police. Following several years of debate about Police accountability, sparked in part by the role of Police during the 1981 South Africa rugby union tour of New Zealand, the Police Complaints Authority was established on 1st April 1989. The Police Complaints Authority comprised a single person, the first Authority being High Court Judge Peter Quilliam.

The Authority had a small group of his own investigators from day one but also relied on the Police to still investigate all "non-serious" and certain "serious" complaints. "Non-Serious" complaints could be simply complaints of rudeness or discourtesy. "Serious" complaints involved allegations of criminal activity by serving Police, including assaults, corruption, sexual offending, thefts, serious driving offending etc. When the Authority was first set up it would forward complaints to the relevant district for investigation, usually by selected Senior Sergeants and Inspectors of both Uniform and Criminal Investigation Branches. There were strict time limits to these enquiries with the need to constantly report to the Authority regularly on progress or otherwise. On occasions one of the Authority's own investigators would also become involved personally overseeing any investigation.

Having been the subject of three internal enquiries myself prior to the establishment of the Authority, one "non-serious" and two "serious" I knew the standard required of the investigating officer was very high indeed.

Whilst most people outside the Police struggle with the concept of the Police investigating their own I can personally provide assurance that such investigations are rigorous and, sadly in my day, aimed more at charging a member of the Police than not.

Two or three of us Senior Sergeants at Whanganui worked for the Authority as required. I always put my Investigators hat on early in any enquiry and then, as it came time to finalise any enquiry I would then put my Prosecutor's hat on. If I charge this cop in Court what are the chances of conviction? What other sanctions can be bought against the cop subject to the enquiry, if any?

Internal enquiries are very time-consuming if they are done right. I would run the enquiry like I would run any enquiry into any person suspected of a criminal offence. Once I had established what had happened and of that, what could be proved to a level where a criminal offence could be alleged in Court, I would then ask to interview the cop or cops involved like any other criminal suspect. The cop or cops had the normal rights of any person to decline the interview or to have counsel present.

After the interview or lack of I would then seek advice about any relevant offences I feel have been committed from the Police Legal Section in National Headquarters in Wellington. This is a group of experienced lawyers, most also serving Police who advise on legal matters nationally for the Police.

Subject to their advice I would then report to the Police Complaints Authority on the outcome of the enquiry and with my recommendations in terms of what, if any, charges could be substantiated and the viability of proceeding to Court or to the Police Tribunal with these charges.

The Authority would then review the whole enquiry file and come back to me with his recommendations for either further enquiry to be done or how to resolve the complaint.

As the Investigating Officer I would also make recommendations on any penalty to be applied where it appears the full sanction of the criminal system is not required but the member(s) involved need to be dealt with within terms of the Police Regulations. This could range from counselling to being charged in a Police Tribunal with the subsequent possibility of dismissal, loss of rank or seniority or a fine.

As in any investigation I would keep in regular contact with the complainant(s) in any internal enquiry, keeping them up to date with progress.

We all usually had at least one of these enquiries each on the go at any one time. Complaints are withdrawn by people at times for various reasons known only to them. Allegations are often found, upon investigation, to be vexatious or just plain false. However there are times when the Police should have done things better and then there are the on-flowing consequences for those involved.

The Authority was good in that it removed any allegations by members that they were being targeted or picked on by senior Police for reasons other than the complaint alleged. The Authority also brought a consistency to the decision-making process, on a national basis, that was missing prior to its establishment. Prior to the Authority's existence it was possible for local District Commanders to target and unfairly treat members for whatever personal reason.

Most internal enquiries under the Authority did not end up in Court but were resolved by a variety of ways. Those matters that went to Court were dealt with as in any other criminal case. Unfortunately the Police, like any large organisation, has its share of bad apples but in my experience it does not take long for them to come to light and moved on, one way or the other.

Chapter 29

Another death of a comrade

Every year, in the warmer months, the Police around New Zealand undertake an operation using helicopters and trucks to locate and seize cannabis growing in the bush. These cannabis plantations are well away from the public access and are sometimes guarded by armed sentries. In my experience the sentries are there more to keep other dope growers away than to take on the Police. Although there have been reports of helicopters being fired upon over the years. I have been involved in AOS operations approaching reported armed sentries at a cannabis plantation but have never found them. We have found evidence of them being there but it seems, luckily for all concerned, once they realise it is the AOS coming they quickly leave the area.

The operation is run from Wellington and each district in New Zealand has a dedicated and experienced group of Police who work on the operation every year. Usually Police with bush or Search and Rescue experience and used to working from helicopters.

There were usually three members of a recovery team. One sitting next to the pilot in the Jet Ranger helicopter and the other two are in the back. All are looking for cannabis when flying over bush areas. Cannabis, not being a native plant, stands out quite well in the New Zealand bush as a brighter green than the native flora. When a plantation is located if the chopper cannot land nearby it will land somewhere close in a paddock or on a ridge and the two spotters in the back will attach themselves to a chain that hangs twenty to twenty five metres below the chopper by way of carabiners and harnesses. The chopper will then slowly lift off with the guys hanging below and fly back to where the cannabis has been located, lowering the two onto the ground near the cannabis. They will then pull the cannabis out of the ground and bundle it for the chopper to take from the site to where the team's vehicles are parked.

This is hard, sweaty and not glamourous work and the team members have to be very fit and hardy individuals.

On 17th December 1990 Detective Tony Harrod fell to his death during a drug recovery operation near Maxwell, north of Whanganui. I was in charge of the drug recovery operation that day and early in the morning bade farewell to Tony, Sgt Garry Patterson and Constable Callum McGillivray when they flew out from Whanganui Airport in the Police helicopter. I remember telling Tony to be careful as he was the oldest member of the team. At about 3.00 pm I was working at Whanganui East Police station, filling in for Garry while he did the drug recovery operation when I received a phone call to say that information had been received that the team was in trouble inland from Waitotara and that one member may be dead.

Upon getting to the main station we managed to find out from the crew that Tony and Callum were on the chain beneath the chopper when Tony moved to adjust himself in the harness and fell seventy feet into the side of a hill. It was clear to the others that he was dead and they were parked on the ridge above. Although they were not hurt they were in no condition to do anything. The Police chopper pilot eventually managed to fly Garry and Callum back to Whanganui. He then flew back to the scene followed by a Whanganui Aero-works chopper flown by Charlie Anderson and with Detective Sergeant Colin Irvine, photographer Sergeant Bill Nicholson and myself as a recovery crew.

The Police pilot guided us to the ridge above the face Tony was lying on but could not do much more due to shock. Garry, Callum and the pilot were overwhelmed with shock and grief. These guys had done this operation for several years together and were very experienced not only at drug recovery but in Search And Rescue and general bushcraft. They were also very close friends.

Upon landing Colin, Bill, Charlie and I went down the face to Tony. We confirmed death and tried to get him up to the ridge. Tony was a big man and we had to carry him about forty metres up to the chopper. It was the hardest and saddest thing I ever had to do as a Police officer. Colin and I managed to get Tony into the stretcher and we all cajoled each other to get him up the face and into the Police chopper. Colin flew back with Tony, Bill and I came back with Charlie. We had to work quick as night was approaching. There were some very emotional moments on the hillside that day.

As the senior NCO on duty I took charge of the actual enquiry. I also had to complete the mortuary procedure on Tony.

While this was going on Detective Sergeant Lindsay Edwards had to find Tony's wife Dallas and tell her. Lindsay and Tony were close friends and this must have been a real test of faith for Lindsay.

Upon our return to the Whanganui station after placing Tony at the morgue the place was in an uproar. It is a small station and Tony was a popular character. The staff was totally devastated. I needed someone to give me a hand with the mortuary procedure. Ideally I wanted an NCO or officer as this would take the responsibility away from the troops. My fellow Senior Sergeants were all tied up with various parts of the operation and could not be spared. The sergeants were likewise busy. Inspector Steve Long from Palmerston North volunteered. I am very experienced in dealing with death in all its shapes and smells but carrying out mortuary procedure on a mate is something else.

Tony being a big man I could not prepare him on my own. Steve was very helpful but at times we were both overwhelmed by the emotion of it all. We managed to clean Tony and hide his injuries prior to Dallas arriving and formally identifying him. It was not so much identification as she and her daughter just wanted to see him. This was about 8.00 p.m. and I eventually found myself back at the Police canteen with a stiff whisky provided by our Regional Commander Assistant Commissioner Alan Galbraith.

I got home late that night and Jenny had already gone to her night shift at our local private hospital. Our fifteen year old Jodie and her brother were in bed asleep. I rang Jen to let her know I was home and broke up over the phone. It had been a very long and very hard day. I remember my young daughter coming out to the kitchen and comforting me, poor kid. Jen came home from work after getting someone to replace her.

The following day I had to attend Tony's post mortem examination as well.

In the days following we had a full Police funeral for Tony and I had an enquiry to run. How did an experienced drug recovery team member fall from a secure harness to his death? We never really satisfied ourselves with an explanation other than the metal clip holding Tony onto the rope mysteriously wound itself open against gravity. The idea was posited that having two people on the one hook may have contributed to the accident. The matter was finalised some months later in the Coroners Court.

At the time Tony fell he was wearing a very nice watch. He did not have this with him when we recovered him. Dallas asked about this. We suspected it had come off in the fall so Lindsay and I flew back to the scene a day or so later, searched the immediate area of bush and found the watch intact and operating. We were able to deliver this to Dallas.

Tony's death was a reason for disillusionment with the Police for me. I had never been keen on drug recovery as a means of controlling the spread of cannabis. It is a thrilling and hard job but I have always advocated spraying. The greenies would not have a bar of this. Better to risk a Police officer's life than possibly damage a few native plants.

The national drug recovery operation was run from Wellington and I was amazed at the lengths one or two key Commissioned Officers took to ensure that no blame came back onto the operation itself for Tony's death. They were almost implying that Tony died through his own carelessness. This was not the case at all. He died because of a freak accident in an operation that is fraught with danger and, I still personally believe, not sustainable on the grounds of safety. The yields of cannabis could be substantial but we all knew we missed far more than we ever got.

Ironic now that we are entering an era where cannabis is becoming less criminalized. Make it legal, tax the growers and the issue would be solved.

Chapter 30

Sex Crimes -The Sad, the Mad and the just plain Bad

One of the least savoury but very important parts of Policing was, in my opinion, investigating allegations of sexual offending. The victim, who has been brave enough to disclose allegations must tell the Police what happened and then, may be required to provide this evidence again in Court with the alleged offender present.

I believe the Police and Court processes are now a lot better than they were when I was a young cop. Victims carry the scar of sexual abuse all their lives. Counselling does help but the scars remain.

Some sexual offending was "victimless". Prior to 1986 homosexual acts between consenting adults was still a crime in New Zealand. Thankfully for a small but significant percentage of our population this is no longer the case.

When I was a nineteen year old freshly minted Constable in Lower Hutt I was working as the watchhouse-keeper one night shift when one of the patrols brought in two very well-dressed men. Both were very articulate, well-presented and refined gentlemen.

The patrol had caught them in a car on the riverside car park in Lower Hutt's commercial area engaged in intercourse. Both were embarrassed and shame-faced. The Daly Street toilets next to the stop-bank and the car park in the then commercial centre of Lower Hutt was a well-known meeting place for homosexuals in those days so certain homophobic Police did also frequent the area trying to catch gays committing crime.

Our Sergeant, the one who did not like Cadets, was ostensibly also a a devout practicing Catholic. He was in the search room while I was processing the two men and he was dishing out a fair bit of tripe to these men about their sexual preferences. One or two others were also contributing. I felt it was unnecessary as these guys were humiliated enough already.

At this stage another cop comes into the search room wearing a Catholic Priest's dog collar. He had been searching the car they were found in and found the collar on the seat. At this the Sergeant lost it. He ordered the cop to take the collar off. He then took one of the men, the one who had identified himself as the car owner and as a priest, to his office, shut the door and that was that.

The priest and his friend were duly charged, processed and bailed to appear in the then Magistrates Court the next week. The Sergeant had contacted someone in authority in the Church with the result that the priest was removed from New Zealand immediately by the Church and did not face any charges. His friend did. **Sad**

I struggled with the hypocrisy of the Sergeant's actions as did a few others on my shift but in those days you kept your trap shut.

A few months later I was driving my patrol car along High Street on a sunny summer afternoon. In those days High Street was the main shopping area of Lower Hutt and the street was busy with families and young couples out for a walk in the beautiful weather. It was a very quiet Sunday afternoon and, as usual, I was wondering about where the next cup of coffee was going to come from. As I drove slowly along a very well-known likely lad, Danny Scotson, came out into the road and stopped me. He was with his wife and young children. I wondered what he wanted. Danny was not a man to engage socially with young cops normally so this was one for the books. He would normally be telling me to fuck off and giving me the fingers.

As I pulled up Danny told me that there was a guy sitting in his car just up the road with no pants on masturbating. He thought that this was a bit rough with all the young families and women walking the streets. I had to agree with him.

I approached the car and there, sure enough, was a middle aged white gent engaged in an act that can apparently cause blindness if over-indulged.

I walked up and opened the driver's door suddenly causing the bloke to just about have a heart attack. We had a bit of a chat about the appropriateness of this behavior in a public street. Well I talked, he just gulped but carried on cranking!

I told him he was under arrest but I wanted his car for forensic testing. I instructed him to drive his car to the nearby Police station and park it in the yard. I told him I would be following him so don't try anything silly. Danny Scotson thought this was wonderful and gave the guy a bit of verbal to go on with.

We got back to the station and I got the guy out of his car, asked him to put his pants on and interviewed, charged and processed the guy for doing an indecent act in a public place. I took his seat covers for the DSIR scientist to look at for seminal stains and put him in the cells overnight for Court the next day. The guy had previous history for indecency so I knew the CIB would want a chat as well. The guy was married with a young family and had no real explanation for his behavior. **Sad**

As a young trainee detective in Wellington in 1975 I was called to a Day Care Centre at the top of Cuba Street. The Centre was in a family home where the owner lived with her husband and young children. Mothers would drop off their very small pre-kindergarten age children to be cared for during the day while they worked.

One of these mothers had called into the office to say that her little girl had told her that the little girl had seen the owner's husband with milk coming out of his diddle while he was sitting on the side of his bed. She told her mother that this was when she and another little girl were in his bedroom.

I spoke to the husband, a very well-presented and well-spoken chap in his mid-thirties, a bit of a man about town sort of chap, three-piece suit and all the trimmings. I told him about the allegations and invited him down to the office for a bit of a chat. By this time another mother had come forward with a similar story. I needed to get this clown to admit his offending due to the very young age of the children. Their evidence was admissible as hearsay but I did not want the children or their families having to go through the Court process for this creep.

I had arranged for a DSIR scientist to examine the area around the suspect's side of the bed and on the floor. Testing revealed acres of human semen on the floor and the furniture around his side of the bed. We interviewed the suspect for some hours before he admitted to his offending. He made a full and frank statement admitting inducing the wee girls to commit indecent acts, and was duly charged with multiple crimes. He pleaded guilty in Court and was sentenced to a lengthy term of imprisonment. Thankfully the families did not have to give evidence which was great. **Bad**

About eleven years later when I was a prosecutor in Whanganui District Court I had to run a depositions hearing prior to trial for a man charged with doing indecent acts upon his own young daughter. Deposition is the taking of evidence, usually in front of two Justices of the Peace, to see if there is enough evidence to establish a prima facie case against an accused. If there is, the accused is then committed to trial in the High Court or District Court.

In walks his Highness, still in a three-piece suit but a bit balder and fatter. His wife and daughter were in the Court precincts as well.
The daughter was about ten or eleven, a baby at the time of the previous episode in Wellington. The daughter gave evidence with the support of her mother. The taking of evidence took all day so at the lunch adjournment the Justices allowed the defendant's bail to continue but told him he must keep away from his daughter and wife.

About an hour later I was walking back to Court when I saw the defendant and his wife walking along the street with their daughter hand-in-hand swinging between them having a great time. All were laughing and enjoying themselves. I advised the Justices that the defendant had broken his bail arrangements. At the end of the depositions hearing the defendant was committed to trial and was remanded in custody pending the trial so that he could not interfere with his child's testimony or influence her. He was found guilty at trial and was sentenced to a very lengthy term on Her Majesty. **Bad and now pretty Mad at not being allowed to go home.**

My first enquiry that resulted in a Supreme (now High) Court trial as the officer in charge of the case occurred while I was a young detective on indecency squad in Wellington in 1976. A fifty six year old woman who lived alone in Brooklyn was raped by a young male after he broke into her home in the middle of the night. We had some items left at the scene by the offender which we managed over a period of time to link to a twenty four year old man who lived nearby in Aro Valley. He was known to the Police for previous sexual offending. He was a refugee, coming to New Zealand from Hungary at the time of the 1956 revolution in that country.

We interviewed the suspect for some hours but he would not make any admissions. We had items that belonged to him found in the victim's home and he denied ever being there. He had no alibi for his whereabouts at the time the crime was committed. We also had a tentative photo identification of the offender by the victim. We went to trial with a case based on circumstantial evidence. For some reason the offender changed his plea to guilty before the trial started and he was sentenced to four years for rape and burglary. **Just plain Bad**

As a postscript to this episode during the enquiry I found that the victim and her children were cousins of mine on my father's side. I had told the boss of this connection as soon as I found out but carried on with the enquiry as Officer in Charge anyway.

When I was in Whanganui in the late eighties I helped set up the then new concept of a Sexual Abuse Team, a joint exercise between the Police and the Children and Young Persons Service. The team would consist of detectives and social workers working together using evidential interviewing techniques when talking to very young children who had allegedly been abused by family or strangers.

The system worked very well but burn out was a constant problem as there is nothing positive in dealing with allegations of sexual abuse within families. You know that this will normally break the family up, usually with one member of the family possibly spending some time in prison.

A child is scarred for life by the offending so great care has to be taken to protect the child from further trauma during any Court process where the crime has to be re-lived.

Getting Detectives and Social Workers to rotate completely on this team does not take long in a small town and not all Police and Social Workers are cut out for this type of work either, thereby reducing the numbers further.

This resulted in a few Detectives and Social Workers who demonstrated the particular skills in dealing with this type of crime being used again and again wearing them out and, in some cases, acting as a catalyst to leave either the Police of the Children & Young Persons Service. There is no easy answer to this problem. I believe that the teams are still run in a similar way and have proved very successful over the years.

Chapter 31

Police Bars

When I joined the Police in 1970 most large Police stations had established Police canteens. These had begun to be set up in the mid to late 1960's I am told. The idea back then was to give Police the chance to have a quiet beer with colleagues without having to be in a public bar watching one's back. It also established a tradition of partners and children being able to meet and also enjoy the Police culture of the time which was, despite what we constantly hear today from people who were not there, a very positive and enjoyable well-behaved environment to be in.

We had the compulsory leaners for the big boys and girls from section and CIB to sit at while they played darts and pool and then tables and chair for older folk and families to sit at. The drinks were cheap and the place was a fun place to be at. The hours were strict but could be extended for special reasons.

This also allowed for a place for the section shift staff to have a quiet beer after their shifts in the early hours of the morning subject to strict rules applied by the Bar Committee, a very powerful little group in every station.

I was a Cadet at the Police College when the first bar was opened there in about 1971. The idea was to allow recruits (Cadets were not allowed in the place) to have a beer after class as in those days most Police recruits came from a civilian working life where they could always have a drink after work if they wanted to. It also kept the recruits out of the local pubs on a Friday night thus stopping them getting into strife that they were not ready for. In those days of long hair Police stood out in pubs and clubs believe me.

Police bars were used as places for post-match social rugby sessions with opposing teams such as other Police teams, the Railways, the Fire Brigade or whatever with a decent feed of saveloys and bread or fish and chips with kids running everywhere drinking soft drinks and scoffing chippies, mums sitting down having a well-earned glass and dads raving on about their (usually imaginary) rugby skills to each other. There were always speeches and presentations. How many young cops learned or honed the art of public speaking in Police Clubs. Some of the best and most entertaining and humourous public speakers I have listened to were older Police, no matter what rank.

When going out socially a lot of cops and their partners met at the Police Canteen for a drink and catch up beforehand. The men all dressed like lounge lizards and the women all dolled up. Great memories.

We got to know each other as friends which really helped on the street. We looked after each other. The bar also acted as the station tea room during day shifts and was also usually set out as a large Operational Emergency Area if needed in times of crisis with all the necessary plugs, jackpoints and sockets installed. It was used as a classroom for probationary staff attending lectures before the unit system of In Service Training started.

Yes we had times when we probably drank too much for our own good but was it not better to do it there rather than in a drinking hole shared by members of the public. There are times in Policing where there is a need to be together in a relaxed environment to deal with what has just happened.

Yes, we did have scrummaging competitions after night shift and other harmless physical activities to let off a bit of steam. Better in the Police club than in a public bar or someone's home. Most sectional Police are young, very fit men and women who do not shy from danger and dares. Goes with the territory that there will be some rambunctious behaviour at times.

However we all knew that sitting in an office not far from us was a Senior Sergeant or duty Sergeant who, whilst trying to turn a deaf ear to what the "kids" are getting up to, also worried that they were overdoing it. At some suitable period a body would arrive at the door bearing stripes or a crown and we would all get the message. Time to go home.

Some not so good things happened in bars at times, the odd knuckle sandwich between guys or an inappropriate comment to or actions towards a member of the fairer sex but in my experience this was usually dealt with firmly by the Bar Committee and the administration. Better there than in the public eye.

Police are not saints. If they were they would not last long. This seems to have been forgotten nowadays. They are men and women who undertake some of the hardest, emotionally gutting and most dangerous tasks in this country along with firemen and women, ambos and medical staff. This tends to make some of them want to play hard. Is it not better to provide them with an environment to do this that is controlled and respected rather than simply closing bars which have been a social centre of most large stations for over fifty years.

A very organised retired copper in my town, Rod Newport, regularly gets together a whole bunch of us old fogies and arranges for the bar at our local Police station to be opened with a barman in attendance. We usually have these meetings at 5.00 p.m. on a Friday night. The bar is opened and off duty Police Officers are there with their families. Us old retired chaps and chapettes are much welcomed by them all and mix in as one would expect. The serving staff patiently listen to our war stories, we drink our low alcohol beers and wines, cups of tea or coffee, or sit on one or two beers for two hours and then all trundle off home for milo and gingernuts at about 7.00 p.m. Brilliant time.

The serving staff and their families are all gone by about 6.15 p.m. We just talk and reminisce as old cops do, pretty harmless really but the comment has been made several times that the heart seemed to have gone out of the place. Some are often heard to say that we would only be getting started at 7.00 p.m. in our day.

I am very sorry to see that, at the time of writing this book, bars are closing around the country and that the bar at the Royal New Zealand Police College has also now closed. I am sure the decision-makers feel that this is happening for the right reasons but....

When Police clubs were first set up New Zealand was a much safer place to be, in terms of attending hotels and clubs, than today. Where do these fit young cops, older settled cops with partners and kids, sporting teams etc. go now?

Chapter 32

Police Partners

I want to give a shout out to the unsung heroes of the Police, the wives, husbands and partners of serving Police.

I was single when I joined the Police, not marrying my darling until I was just rwenty one and her nineteen. This was very young by today's standards but not by the standards of the times. Our marriage has stayed the distance, something for which I am very grateful. Jenny has been my rock over the years, especially during some of the times in the Police when things were getting a bit tough and weird. Many a lesser woman would have walked out on me and I would not have blamed her.

Partners are there to meet you at the end of a horrible day, listen to your war stories if you are of a mind to share them, put up with you coming home late after "de-briefing" in the bar, put up with the sometimes social isolation of being married to a cop, running the home and family for long periods of time while you are away on operations or at the Police college on courses.

In small stations wives, husbands and partners have to step up to take messages for their loved one, ring for assistance, feed a prisoner, put up with members of the public coming to the house all hours of the night and day to report issues and at the same time maintain a certain image in town as the cop's partner.

When I finished in the Police Jen and I had been married for nineteen years and I worked out that I had been away from home for nearly four years of that time on Police business or courses. I have no idea how our marriage survived.

Subsequent to leaving the Police I have made it my business to either be home all the time or to, wherever possible, take Jenny with me when away on business.

My experience is no different to thousands of other Police, both serving and now retired. Our partners put up with a lot because of what we chose or choose to do for a career. Children are also affected by Dad or Mum being a copper. Just ask them what their times were like at school when they are older and you may be shocked to hear what they had to put up with, especially in smaller towns or districts.

Being a cop changes an individual. I saw this a bit over the years when older married people joined the Police. Their partners would often comment that they had changed. Mostly things worked out but sometimes the cop had choices to make.

If I was ever privileged enough to be asked by a cop what he or she should do when things are not going well at home I would usually say being a cop is really only a job, being a wife or husband or father/mother is a life-long duty and privilege – you sort out what is important to you and make the decision and learn to live with it. You can always get another job.

Chapter 33

Time to go

The seven years I served in AOS was, overall, fun. Great bunch of people, some scary times, plenty of laughs, a few frights but I would not have missed it for the world. I was starting to question why I was in the Police at about this time. I enjoyed being a Senior Sergeant but could not see myself doing it forever. I did not want to leave Whanganui on further promotion, being an inspector working shifts in Auckland or Wellington having no appeal to me. We had a large circle of friends outside the Police and we liked Whanganui.

Since 1981 I had had problems sleeping. This seemed to be an outcome of the Jack Enquiry that I had to learn to live with. In 1987, whilst working in the CIB, I felt really out of touch and down. I went to my GP and he diagnosed depression and put me on medication for a few months. The side effects were not pleasant but I started sleeping well again which was a plus. I had taken a couple of weeks off work as well which seemed to settle me.

During 1991 I took another spell of sick leave. I was not myself. My doctor diagnosed clinical depression or the "black dog" again and referred me to a psychiatrist, Dr Jana Fernando. I was tired all the time, irritable and an arse to live with. Jana was amazed it had taken me so many years to seek support. She explained that I had depression, probably since childhood and that this was caused by the high levels of anxiety I felt as a child at home. I had explained to her that, as a teenager, on a couple of occasions, I had emotional breakdowns for some unknown reason. Once was at home and Mum helped me through it and once was in the Police Cadets when a couple of my mates were there for me.

Jana set out the number of "critical incidents" that I had been through in my life going back to witnessing the assaults on Mum when I was a small child, any one of which was enough to trigger serious mental health issues in many individuals. It was a sobering experience to listen to. She said she saw this a lot in serving Police at the time and was not surprised that when wheels fall off for cops they fall off in style. The wish to persevere and carry on as if nothing has happened was very strong in cops in those days. Depression did not have the recognition it has now and most were ashamed to be diagnosed with it. I know I was.

Jana was surprised at the resilience of cops who she saw, but usually too late in the process to save their careers.

However I managed to get myself together and returned to duty later in 1991. It was not the same. I felt like a stranger and did not really feel like a Police Officer.   I persevered and managed to cope. I was torn between leaving a job that I loved, leaving the security and reasonable income and starting over again at thirty nine years of age with a mortgage and young family. I had the respect of my peers, bosses and staff but I felt out of place. I was still doing a good job as a Senior Sergeant running staff training, prosecuting, supervising general police operations, doing gang liaison work, undertaking staff enquiries etc., but my heart was not in it.

I was becoming disillusioned with the way the Police was developing, the merging of the MOT with the Police was one issue I struggled with. It has settled down now of course but the merger did not get off to a good start with Ministry Of Transport staff coming over to the Police with equivalent rank, having never trained as Police or sat exams for promotion. There was some resentment from both sides.

I counted and still count amongst my friends ex MOT guys so this was not personal. I simply struggled with the cynical way the government of the day (John Banks) added 1000 new members to the Police. Many ex MOT guys have gone on to high promotion in the Police or have continued in the Police as a career on the street and I applaud them for that.

I began to plan my departure. I had always had problems sleeping, possibly due to shift work, but lack of sleep, long hours, and some disaffection in what I was doing combined to make me a sad boy. This was not helped by some really serious stuff I had been involved in over the years, stuff a lot of cops have to deal with but can become cumulative if not addressed appropriately. In my day it was dealt with by trying to ignore it or, worse, trying to drink it away. Counselling was in its infancy in the Police and not readily accessed by us.

During my Police career I received more than my share of injuries, both physical and psychological. I always liked the excitement of the job. I also liked to make tough decisions but these can backfire at times. I needed to get out of the Police, to move on. In March 1992 I let the Police know I was applying to retire on the ground of physical and psychological illness.

My then District Commander, John Thurston, could not have

been more supportive. He offered me two years of leave without pay and a transfer to anywhere after that. Whilst I was very grateful for this option it was not a realistic choice for a man with a very young family to make. We had a big mortgage which still had be paid and I would need to get another job just to support us. Also we would likely need to leave Whanganui at the end of the two years as there was no guarantee of my position still being here for me.

My childhood asthma was back and not getting any better which did not help when chasing crims or struggling with prisoners. I was pretty much burnt out. Jana managed to talk me through this process. She explained that I had had over twenty two years of pretty hard policing and it was catching up. For personal reasons I did not want to leave Whanganui and did not want to be a Senior Sergeant for another nine or ten years just to get a pension. I went on sick leave in about March 1992 and finished in the Police on 30 June that year.

I still miss the job every day but am accepting that it was no longer for me. Like many jobs being a cop is a really hard existence but overall, it was also all just great fun with some scary, sad, frightening and sobering experiences thrown in. Work never held the same attraction to me after the Police but I had to make a living which I did well. I still live with the "black dog" unfortunately but manage it well.

Chapter 34

The last instalment of "My Brilliant Career" (yeh right)

It is many years now since I left the Police. I still have many fond memories of the job and the really fine good people I worked with and have not joined the "disaffected coppers' club" which a few of my ex-colleagues tend to find themselves in for some reason. No one made us do it for goodness sake.

I admire and thoroughly support the Police and think it is one of the best jobs a young person can do both for their community and for their personal development. Like all large organisations the Police has its faults, but they are far outnumbered by the examples of good work carried out every day by men and women who step up to make a difference, helping and protecting those who cannot help or protect themselves, have a strong vocation and dedication to their oath. God bless you, New Zealand should be proud to have one of the best, if not the best, and most honest Police Departments in the world.

My first job after the Police was working for an old mate, Steve Taylor, a barrister. I trained as a legal executive and worked as Steve's barrister's clerk. I did most of the preparation work for criminal trials, for the defence this time. Steve was an ex Police Cadet who had left prior to graduating due to some high-jinks relating to dance-halls and selling grog. He then went to University and studied law. He always regretted leaving the Police and retains close links with Police wherever he is.

Working for "the other side" did not hamper my relations with old mates from the Police in general. A certain few younger cops displayed some distance though. I guess they felt I had turned bad or something. Checking Police evidence for trials as a member of the defence team was, generally, disheartening professionally as the Police usually did a very good job.

However on the odd occasion I was very disappointed in the lack of depth of enquiry undertaken by Police prior to shoving someone into Court. The defence naturally got a copy of all the Police evidence prior to trial so I would go and re-interview some witnesses or actually interview witnesses the Police had not bothered with. On one occasion this resulted in a defendant, a very well-known and dangerous criminal, walking free after facing very serious charges including kidnapping. I found witnesses who gave him an alibi and who would give evidence. I presented these witnesses to the Police after taking my own statements, asking them to check them out and decide what they wanted to do. The Officer in Charge of the trial decided to persevere with the charges. The defendant was found not guilty by the jury and walked out of the Court a free man. The defendant is a thug and a brute but on this occasion the Police did not do their job properly. I took no pleasure in the outcome but, as I did say to the cop in charge of the trial he had a chance to follow up after me providing him with the other witnesses who we later called for the defence but he chose not to. We were never that close after this for some reason.

After about two years I left Steve's, not enough work really for me, and began working for Whanganui Insurance Brokers as a claims officer and trainee broker. This was not very well paid but a very happy place to work. I only lasted about six months but learnt a lot.

I had applied for a job at ACC in Whanganui as a Team Leader. Surprisingly I got the position. Upon starting I was given the fraud liaison officer's role. In those days ACC had a fraud rep in every branch who liaised with contracted investigators, all ex-Police. This was one of many jobs I had been applying for as I really felt the need to increase my income.

This job turned out to be a new career and calling for me. I eventually, after a restructuring, became a Case Manager. ACC then sent me to university for a year to complete a Post Graduate diploma in Health Science, graduating from university at the age of forty seven!!

The university had, upon my application for the course, recognized my previous Police and Law Society exams and legal training together with work experience as the equivalent of an undergraduate degree and admitted me to the post graduate programme at the Auckland Medical School. I did the seven full time papers in twelve months as well as carrying on with a challenging caseload. The diploma concentrated on industrial diseases and Traumatic Brain Injury rehabilitation. I had no free weekends at all that year but Jenny was a great help as she had just finished her nursing degree and was able to help me with the research needed etc. I also had to spend lengthy tutorials in Auckland during the year. I returned to work at ACC and continue to manage clients with TBI and clients who were just plain bad boys and girls or unable to be managed by female staff.

In 2008 I applied for a role in the new National Serious Injury Service in ACC, getting the role due to my work with clients with brain injury, spinal cord injury and other serious long term injuries. It is sometimes funny how life works out. I would never have picked doing this kind of work when I was a cop.

I guess growing up with a sister who suffered a very severe traumatic brain injury at birth instilled in me the compassion and empathy to enable me to work with clients who are severely disabled. Not all Case Managers can do this as the work is extremely challenging at times for obvious reasons. My role was to ensure that my clients and their families were able to access ALL the services provided by ACC and rehabilitation was put in place to enable them to reach their potential in life.

In 2015, at the age of sixty three I was sitting at my computer at work having just finished a meeting with my manager. I had made a small oops in our privacy policy, accidentally e-mailing a message to the wrong client. I knew I had done it as soon as it happened, contacted the client and he deleted it. I then contacted the right client, told him what I had done and sent him the message. All good. The clients understood, having been clients for many years and knowing the pressure we worked under.

I then told my manager what had happened. She was then bound to advise Human Resources, culminating in me receiving a twelve month warning with instant dismissal if this occurred again. This was not an unusual occurrence in the frenetic atmosphere we worked in but most did not tell their managers. This is a two edged sword as if they are found out they are summarily dismissed. My manager was as upset as I was but that's the rules. I had worked for the same employer for over twenty years looking after up to about ninety clients and families at any one time with very high needs most of that time. I enjoyed my role and really enjoyed working with my clients. I was very well-rewarded and really have no gripe with the ACC as the working conditions in my contract were great. Just a sign of the times we now live in.

Whilst sitting at my desk I looked around at my colleagues beavering away, all doing their best to try to make people's lives a little easier. Most were young females, most university-educated, all very bright and articulate and great to work with. I then looked at my older colleagues, again mostly female but a few old guys, all with a lifetime of public service behind them, straight from school in the late 60's and early 70's, for some university happening later in life when the kids were a bit older. All very bright and very experienced. I count myself privileged to have known them all.

I thought enough is enough. I have worked full time since leaving school at seventeen for mainly two employers, working with people in crisis for forty six years. I finished university at forty seven after our youngest had left home. Jenny had done her nursing degree in her forties as well. We had raised two successful kids, worked our buns off to get our own home, both working long hours and relying on family to provide child support at times. My health was suffering due to the hours I was working and the travel involved. I am out of here. I let my manager know that I planned to retire on 1 April 2016. She was genuinely upset but very supportive and, I think, a wee bit jealous!! I made sure I did not make any further little oops on the computer for the months remaining, spent time saying good-bye to clients, had a nice morning tea on the day I left and retired at sixty three. I had mixed feelings but I knew my position would be taken by another very clever younger person who needs the job, very high paying but very challenging. Unfortunately they took the position away from the town I live in and filled it at a metropolitan office. Another job lost in our small city.

This was one of the best decisions I had ever made. My health instantly improved. My time was my own for the first time since I was a carefree schoolboy. I am lucky in that I have always been able to occupy myself so I find the days slip by. The house is now re-painted, we have done the obligatory OE, I have organised several reunions of past work mates, my third form class and family. I am a really busy guy. I also returned to writing, a passion I have had most of my life but with never the time to indulge. We have to watch the pennies but we are used to that – see above. We have managed to travel overseas a bit in the last fifteen years after the kids had left home so travel is not a priority for us. This gives us more ability to fund other interests. I highly recommend retirement if this is an option for people. I know we are very fortunate and others may not be as lucky so this makes me more thankful.

I am very proud and privileged to have met most of my clients and their families. They live with life-long adversity and uncertainty due to very serious injuries. I was very proud to receive cards and e-mails from some of my families when I retired telling me how much I meant to them. I can now count them as friends, not clients.

Jenny retired from nursing four years before I retired. Our children are both independent and have good jobs, Jodie as a rehabilitation coach at a special care unit for people in Whanganui with traumatic brain injury and Luke as a Police Officer in Wellington. The apples did not fall far from the tree!!

ACC provided me with a new career, albeit at a somewhat slower pace, thank goodness.

I now fussle and pootle as a retired lady or gent should, organizing reunions, writing "rubbish", gardening, reading, drinking fine wine and cooking fine food, watching all sport, using MySky, spending more time than is appropriate for a person of my age on social media (in a nice way), taking two years to paint the house, offering advice to all the super rugby coaches and Shag on selections and tactics from my Lay Z Boy whether they like it or not, organizing "holiday breaks" for the bride and myself either in New Zealand or overseas, keeping in touch with some of the best people this country has produced and generally finding not enough hours in the day to get "things" done. I have no idea how I managed to fit work in.

www.ingramcontent.com/pod-product-compliance
Lightning Source LLC
Chambersburg PA
CBHW050110280326
41933CB00010B/1046